TYRANNY-BUSTERS

Tyranny-Busters

The Sham and Shame of the Federal Income Tax

Michael Benoit

Michael Benoit Publishing
San Diego California

Michael Benoit
8781 Cuyamaca St. Ste D,
Santee, Ca. 92071

Printed in the United States of America
Signature Book Printing, www.sbpbooks.com
First edition: June 2008
Second edition: November 2012
ISBN 978-0-9818144-0-7

CONTENTS

Preface

The Tyranny Busters series are dedicated to Thomas Jefferson and to Otto Skinner. I consider Thomas Jefferson to be one of the greatest tyranny busters to have ever lived; and Otto Skinner will be, if his work can eventually be understood and widely disseminated. In the quotes shown below, volumes are spoken on the subject and are encapsulated for our consumption.

Just take one pill three times daily, to fight tyranny!

"I have sworn upon the altar of God, eternal hostility against every form of tyranny over the mind of man"

- Thomas Jefferson

Jefferson is responsible for spreading thousands of seeds of liberty, but for me, the seed quoted above is so important that it becomes a pillar of liberty. If this were all that Jefferson ever wrote, it would still be of monumental significance.

"What is it that is actually being taxed? Is it people? Is it property? Or is it activities? There cannot be any intelligent conversation about a tax until the actual subject of the tax is known."

Otto Skinner

Only after you either apply this knowledge, or insist on getting answers to these questions (in regards to the so-called "income" tax), will you finally understand the mental tyranny under which Americans have been laboring. If we were to get an answer to these questions, the next question Otto poses is this: "In what section, if any, of the Internal Revenue Code does it impose a tax on that particular subject?"

A tyranny over the mind of man embodies the essence of slavery, complete with the ignorance of being enslaved by the enslaver. A tyranny over a mind is tantamount to mind control, and is also suppression of the highest order. With the Tyranny Busters series, I attempt to do my part to remove some of the tyranny that currently exists over the mind of man. One day, may freedom prevail!

Thank you, Thomas Jefferson and Otto Skinner! Thank you Dann for all your help in editing this piece for me.

INTRODUCTION

The Tyranny Busters books are written with the purpose of freeing minds from tyranny. Thomas Jefferson's quote below caused me to give this subject a long, hard look. I have been enlightened by this simple quote of Jefferson's, and I hope that I may enlighten others as he continues to do throughout the ages.

What did Thomas Jefferson mean when he wrote, "I have sworn upon the altar of God, eternal hostility against every form of tyranny over the mind of man."? Why did he say "...over the mind of man"?

Did he conceive tyranny to mean only despotic rule? If so, why did he say "...every form of tyranny"?

He was speaking of tyranny over the mind, not over the body. Why? Why was this kind of tyranny so disagreeable to him? In ancient Greece, tyranny referred to a government that took power without the right to do so—to rule without right, whether benevolent or despotic. To control a person's mind without their awareness is, in my opinion, the ultimate tyranny. It is this form of tyranny that I wish to address.

Controlling minds through fraud is a common practice of governments. This fraud is accomplished through propaganda and with repeated lies. Today, our government has almost convinced us that we would starve if not for its benevolent care. The tyranny I address in this book is the so-called Federal "Income" Tax. Our government has convinced us that we must, in effect, subject ourselves to slavery in order to be free. What a tyranny this is upon our minds!

To stimulate your brain a little, ask yourself these questions: "Do you, as an individual, have inalienable rights? Do you have the inalienable 'right' to the preservation of life and liberty? Do you own yourself? Does the 'right' to the preservation of life depend on the permission or control of government? Does the government have the power to determine how much of your labor will be forfeited to the state? Can a 'right' be taxed? Do you have a 'right' to your own sanity?"

What is sanity? We know that when people are deemed to be insane, they are thought to be not responsible for their actions. So, those who are responsible for their actions must therefore be 'sane'. If there is tyranny over a mind, then that mind is neither sane, nor free, nor responsible for itself.

Think about this concept for a minute: when this country began, the people were neither dependent on the government for their existence, nor was their labor confiscated by the government. This country began with the premise that we all had an inalienable right to life, liberty and the pursuit of happiness, and that those rights could not be taken from us – in whole or part.

In the Declaration of Independence, Jefferson wrote that governments were instituted among men to secure our rights. Is that what our government does today, when it requires that many of us give up great portions of our property and/or labor for the benefit of those whom politicians deem fit to reward?

It is time to remove some tyranny from our minds and to restore personal liberty and individual responsibility to our fair land.

Mike Benoit, Author

CHAPTER ONE

CONSTITUTIONAL TAXATION AND INTERPRETATIONS THEREOF, BY THE SUPREME COURT

"What is it that is actually being taxed? Is it people? Is it property? Or is it activities? There cannot be any intelligent conversation about a tax until the actual subject of the tax is known."

Otto Skinner

The Constitution of the United States has provided Congress with the power of taxation, or to impose a tax. The Supreme Court has referred to this power as a *plenary power*, which means:

Webster's Dictionary, 1828 Edition

"PLE'NARY, a. [L. plenus.]
Full; entire; complete; as a plenary license; plenary consent; plenary indulgence. The plenary indulgence of the pope is an entire remission of penalties to all sins."

I will be using the 1828 Webster's Dictionary for definitions, whenever possible, so that we will have the same meaning that the Founding Fathers assigned to these words, except for any words that entered the Constitution at a later date.

Congress has a plenary power of taxation; therefore, Congress can do whatever it chooses, right? Not exactly! We will soon learn that some strings are attached which actually bind this power. These details stipulate that Congress must follow some clear rules regarding this plenary power of taxation.

Before we explore these rules, we will review some definitions of the words used within these rules, or grants of power. The power of Congress that relates to taxation is contained in three short sections of the Constitution, which contain the following words:

- *tax*
- *impost*
- *duty*
- *excise*
- *direct*
- *indirect* (not in the Constitution, but necessary to understand the *direct* tax)
- *apportion*
- *uniform*
- *capitation*
- *custom*

The words above must be completely understood in order to fully comprehend the power of taxation that has been granted to Congress. Let us begin with the definition of the word *tax*.

"TAX, n. [L. taxo, to tax.]

    1. A rate or sum of money assessed on the person or property of a citizen by government, for the use of the nation or state. Taxes, in free governments, are usually laid upon the property of citizens according to their income, or the value of their estates. Tax is a term of general import, including almost every species of imposition on persons or property for supplying the public treasury, as tolls, tribute, subsidy, excise, impost, or customs. But

more generally, tax is limited to the sum laid upon polls, lands, houses, horses, cattle, professions and occupations. So we speak of a land tax, a window tax, a tax on carriages, &c. Taxes are annual or perpetual.

2. A sum imposed on the persons and property of citizens to defray the expenses of a corporation, society, parish or company; as a city tax, a county tax, a parish tax, and the like. So a private association may lay a tax on its members for the use of the association."

To fully understand the subject of taxation, we will first divide all taxes into two categories: the first being *direct* taxes, the second being *indirect* taxes. All federal taxes belong in either one category or the other.

"DIRECT, a. [L., to make straight. See Right.]:

Direct tax, is a tax assess on real estate, as houses and lands."

INDIRECT', a. [L. indirectus; in and directus, from dirigo.]

5. Indirect tax is a tax or duty on articles of consumption, as an excise, customs, &c."

From what you have learned so far, can you determine whether an *impost* tax is a *direct* or indirect tax? Now we will look at the definitions of some more words that are from within the Constitution.

"IM'POST, n. [L. impositum, impono.]

1. Any tax or tribute imposed by authority; particularly, a duty or tax laid by government on goods imported, and paid or secured by the importer at the time of importation. Imposts are also called customs."

"DUTY, n.:

7. Tax, toll, impost, or customs; excise; any sum of money required by government to be paid on the importation, exportation, or consumption of goods. An impost on land or other real estate, and on the stock of farmers, is not called a duty, but a direct tax."

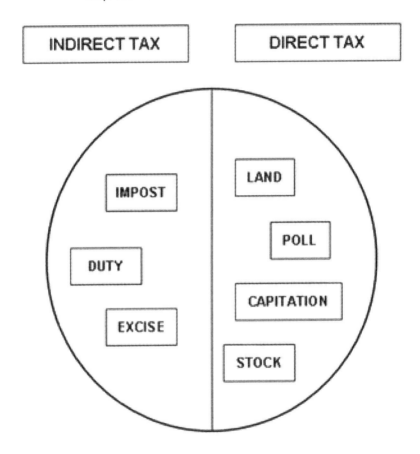

After reading the definition of *duty,* can you tell whether or not a *duty* is an *indirect* tax? You may have some confusion because under the definition of *impost,* we read that an *impost* can be any tax or tribute imposed by an authority; then we read that it is particularly a tax on imported goods, which is also called a *custom.* When we use the term *impost,* generally we mean it as a *custom,* not as a tax in the general sense.

A *duty* refers to a tax that is imposed on some sort of <u>activity</u>; a tax on real estate or a tax on a farmers' stock is not a *duty,* but is instead a *direct* tax.

> **"EXCI'sE, n. s as z. [L. excisum, cut off, from excido.]**
> An inland duty or impost, laid on commodities consumed, or on the retail, which is the last state before consumption; as an excise on coffee, soap, candles, which a person consumes in his family. But many articles are excised at the manufactories, as spirit at the distillery, printed silks and linens at the printer's, &c."

Notice that the reference to *duty* defines *excise*; also notice that an *excise* is an inland *duty.* Remember that a *duty* is <u>not</u> a *direct* tax. Therefore, it must be an *indirect* tax. It is also important to note that an *excise* tax is laid on <u>consumed commodities</u>. Where do you think *excise* taxes belong—in the *direct* category, or the *indirect* category?

> **"APPO'RTIONED,**
> Divided; set out or assigned in suitable parts or shares."

If we *apportion* the food among the number of people at the table, it means that the food will be divided—and that each person at the table will receive a share, or a percentage of the food. The food may be apportioned in different ways, e.g., apportioned according to size with larger people getting larger portions.

"U'NIFORM a. [L. uniformis; unus, one, and forma, form.]
    1. Having always the same form or manner; not variable."

"CAPITATION, n.
    1. Numeration by the head; a numbering of persons.
    2. A tax, or imposition upon each head or person; a poll-tax.
        Sometimes written Capitation-tax."

Shortly, you will see that the Constitution calls a *capitation* tax a *direct* tax. Hopefully, we now have an understanding about which taxes are *direct* and which are *indirect*. If we are unsure about the category of a tax item, we need to review these definitions to determine if we are dealing with an *impost* tax, an *excise* tax, a *custom* tax, a *duty* tax, or a *direct* tax. If you review these definitions, you will find that *indirect* taxes are imposed on <u>activities</u> or <u>privileges</u>, and *direct* taxes are imposed on <u>people</u> or <u>property</u>.

Now, let us review some sections of the Constitution itself, where we will find the rules and grants of powers to which Congress must adhere when passing legislation that involves taxation.

UNITED STATES CONSTITUTION

"Article I, Section 2.,Clause 3.
    Representatives and direct Taxes shall be apportioned among the several States, which may be included within this Union, according to their respective Numbers...""

This is the first place in the Constitution where a restriction is laid on the power of Congress to tax.

Direct taxes <u>must</u> be *apportioned*. Many of us become confused when we try to understand the meaning of a tax that is *apportioned* among the states. It does <u>not</u> mean that each <u>person</u> pays a portion of the tax. Do you remember the previous example about a number of people at the table who receive a larger portion of the food? With an *apportioned* tax, the states that have a greater number of people also have a larger portion of the tax liability. Each state's tax assessment is equal to the percentage of the population within the state, compared to the population of the United States. The bill is *apportioned* among the states, not among the people.

For example: Congress passes a direct tax that calls for a billion dollars. Each state's portion of that bill is then calculated according to the percentage of the population in that state, compared to the total population of the United States. California has about 12 percent of the total population, so its share of the tax bill is about 120 million dollars. Apportionment does not mean that each person will pay a portion of this tax. The Constitution stipulates that the tax is apportioned among the states, not among the people.

Many of us become too concerned about how a tax will be collected or paid. Actually, however, this is not an issue, since it does not matter whether the check is written from the State Treasury, whether the state collects the tax, or whether the Federal Government assesses and collects the tax. The key issue is this: if the tax is *direct*, then the Federal government must *apportion* the tax among the states according to their population. The Federal government must also state the amount of the tax it intends to collect, because there must be a quantifiable number before any *apportionment* can occur.

During your history of being taxed, do you remember if the Federal Government has ever apportioned any tax among the states?

Now we will return to our review of the Constitution.

"Article 1, Section 8.

The Congress shall have Power To lay and collect Taxes, Duties, Imposts and Excises, to pay the Debts and provide for the common Defense and general Welfare of the United States; but all Duties, Imposts and Excises shall be uniform throughout the United States;"

In Section 8, the Congress is provided with a plenary power to tax, however a restriction about *indirect* taxes is also imposed. These taxes—*duties*, *imposts* and *excises* (*indirect* taxes) must be uniform. Notice that a *duty*, *impost* and an *excise* are taxes which are not imposed on <u>property</u> or <u>people</u>, but instead are applied to an <u>event</u>.

> **"Article 1, Section 9., Clause 4**
> No Capitation, or other direct, Tax shall be laid, unless in Proportion to the Census or Enumeration herein before directed to be taken."

Clause 4 above iterates the prohibition imposed on Congress to not lay any *direct* tax without *apportionment*. The first mention of this prohibition is shown in Article 1 Section 2. Congress is prohibited from imposing a *direct* tax without an *apportionment*. Therefore, it is clear that no *direct* taxes are allowed without *apportionment*.

As you can see, *direct* taxes must be apportioned according to the population, and other taxes (*indirect*) must be uniform throughout the United States. These are the only rules or restrictions that I have found in the Constitution about the power of Congress to impose a tax.

Under the rules of apportionment, Congress must determine the amount of money that is needed (apportionment, or division, must begin with the total amount). Then Congress must divide the bill according to the census population (the percentage of people in each state). Although we have 50 states, the apportionment would not be 2% for each state. California has about 12% of the population, so its share of the bill would be 12% of the total amount.

Currently, are any taxes imposed on us apportioned?

For *indirect* taxes, we have the rule of <u>uniformity</u>. Congress cannot impose a different rate of tax in one area of the country than it imposes on the rest of the country. It must be <u>uniform</u>.

We know the rules now, so how do we know a *direct* tax from an *indirect* tax? Let's see what the authorities tell us. Always remember that *direct* taxes must be <u>apportioned</u> and *indirect* taxes must be <u>uniform</u>.

Ah, you say, but the Sixteenth Amendment changed all that. It did not change that! And here's why.

> **"Amendment XVI**
>> The Congress shall have power to impose and collect taxes on incomes, from whatever source derived, without apportionment among the several States, and without regard to any census or enumeration."

Brushaber v. Union Pacific Railroad Co., 240 U.S. 1, 16-17 (1916)

> "The conclusion reached in the Pollock case… recognized the fact that taxation on income was, in its nature, an excise…"

Stanton v. Baltic Mining (240 U.S. 103), 1916

> ". . . by the previous ruling it was settled that **the provisions of the Sixteenth Amendment <u>conferred no new power of taxation</u> but simply prohibited the previous complete and plenary power of income taxation possessed by Congress from the beginning from being taken out of the category of indirect taxation to which it inherently belonged and being placed in the category of direct taxation.**" [emphasis added]

The Stanton case above references both *direct* and *indirect* taxation, and it also specifies that the Sixteenth Amendment **<u>conferred no new power on Congress</u>**. It recognized that from the beginning, Congress had the **<u>power to tax incomes, but that this form of taxation could only be an *indirect* tax.</u>** Upon what person, property, or activity can *indirect* taxes be imposed? Are they imposed on property or people, or on revenue taxable activities? Can an *indirect* tax be imposed on the right to life?

In the above Stanton quote, we are told that the Sixteenth Amendment <u>prohibited income taxation</u> <u>from being removed from the category of *indirect* taxation.</u> The Tyler case quoted on page 24 states, "A tax laid upon the happening of an event, as distinguished from its tangible fruits, is an indirect tax." Please also note that the Brushaber case quoted above states, " . . . taxation on income was, in its nature, an excise . . ." All of these cases clarify that <u>income</u> is not the <u>subject</u> of any tax, but is instead the <u>measure</u> of a tax imposed on a <u>revenue</u> <u>taxable</u> <u>activity</u>.

Assuming that there is an income tax, into which category would it fall: *indirect* or *direct*?

Would an income tax be a tax on <u>property</u>, or would it be a tax related to some <u>activity</u>?

What else does the Supreme Court say about *direct* and *indirect* taxes?

Flint v. Stone Tracy Co., 220 U.S. 107, 119 (1911)

"Any tax when placed on the right of the man or of the corporation to live is a capitation tax and as direct as any tax can be."

We know that Congress can place a tax on the right to life, but such a tax according to the Flint case above is a *direct* tax. So could Congress place an indirect tax on the right to live? The answer is given in Flint vs. Stone above. The answer is <u>no</u>, as that form of tax would be a *capitation* tax and as *direct* as any tax could ever be. Do some of you want to continue to believe that the so-called income tax is a *direct* tax?

If income (property) were the subject of the income tax, then it would be a *direct* tax on <u>property</u>. But, you say, it <u>is</u> a *direct* tax. Well, if it is, then where is the <u>apportionment</u>? We must conclude that the so-called income tax is an *indirect* tax, and as such is imposed either on a privilege or on some other taxable activity.

Flint v. Stone Tracy Co., 220 U.S. 107 (1911):

"**Excises are taxes laid upon the manufacture, sale or consumption of commodities within the country, upon licenses to pursue certain occupations and upon corporate privileges . . . the requirement to pay such taxes involves the exercise**

of privileges, and the element of absolute and unavoidable demand is lacking . . .

. . . It is therefore well settled by the decisions of this court that when the sovereign authority has exercised the right to tax a legitimate subject of taxation as an exercise of a franchise or privilege, it is no objection that the measure of taxation is found in the income produced in part from property which of itself considered is nontaxable . . .

Conceding the power of Congress to tax the business activities of private corporations . . . the tax must be measured by some standard . . . " [emphasis added]

Now in Flint v. Stone Tracy Co., the puzzle unwinds more as we learn that Congress can lay a tax on an **exercise of a franchise** or **privilege, can also label it as an income tax,** and can thereby use income as a means to measure the tax.

A tax on personal property is a *direct* tax. If a franchise or privilege is the subject of the tax (*excise*) then it is an *indirect* tax. For example, if it is a corporation then it does not matter if the corporation has property and receives income from that property, since the income or property is not the subject of the tax. The tax is measured by the income of an activity that Congress has chosen to tax (a taxable activity).

If Congress had imposed a tax on income (that is, on *property* known to us as money), and if that property were the subject of the tax (not a tax on a corporation or on a taxable activity) then the tax would be **void for lack of apportionment,** as that would make it **a *direct* tax**. We are left with no option but to conclude, absent any apportionment, that no direct taxes exist at the present time.

Is the activity in which you are engaged considered by the Constitution to be a revenue taxable activity? Or is the money you receive from that activity the subject of the tax on which you pay your income tax?

U.S. Supreme Court TYLER v. U.S., 281 U.S. 497 (1930)

"A tax laid upon the happening of an event, as distinguished from its tangible fruits, is an indirect tax . . ."

Do you understand that the so-called income tax we are discussing here is <u>not</u> a *direct* tax, but is, instead, a form of *indirect* tax, since there is no apportionment? This tax is not imposed on the fruits of your labor; instead, the occurrence of an <u>event</u> is the subject of this form of taxation.

Do you also understand that the money we receive from our labor is <u>property</u> and, as such, is not the **subject** of any tax? However, it can be the *measure* of a tax if it flows from a revenue taxable activity.

POLLOCK v. FARMERS' LOAN AND TRUST COMPANY. No. 893. SUPREME COURT OF THE UNITED STATES 157 U.S. 429; 15 S. Ct. 673; 1895

"First. We adhere to the opinion already announced, that, taxes on real estate being indisputably direct taxes, taxes on the rents or income of real estate are equally direct taxes.

Second. We are of opinion that taxes on personal property, or on the income of personal property, are likewise direct taxes.

Third. The tax imposed by sections twenty-seven to thirty-seven, inclusive, of the act of 1894, so far as it falls on the income of real estate and of personal property, being a direct tax within the meaning of the Constitution, and therefore unconstitutional and void because not apportioned according to representation, all those sections, constituting one entire scheme of taxation, are necessarily invalid."

In the Pollock case cited above, what strikes me is the unequivocal language clearly specifying that taxes on personal property, and the income from personal property, are both described as *direct* taxes.

Therefore, I conclude that both labor and the property produced by labor are personal property. Since neither labor nor the properties produced by labor can be the subject of any tax (because these taxes are not apportioned), then this tax must be, in its nature, a form of *indirect* tax that is imposed on specific activities or privileges. The nature of these activities remains to be seen.

"Therefore, the income tax is not a tax on income as such. It is an *excise* tax with respect to certain activities and privileges that are measured by the amount of income that they produce. The income is not the subject of the tax; instead, it is the basis for determining the amount of tax." Refer to the **House Congressional Record, 3-27-43, page 2580.**

Now it is quiz time, and this is an open book test.

1. Is the so-called income tax a *direct* tax?
2. Is the so-called income tax *apportioned*?
3. Is it property that is being taxed by the so-called income tax?
4. Is it possible for income to be the item we use to measure a tax, but is not actually the subject of the tax?
5. What subjects can be taxed as an *excise* tax?
6. Is an *excise* tax a *direct* tax?
7. Is an *excise* tax an *indirect* tax?
8. Does an *indirect* tax have to be apportioned?
9. Did the Sixteenth Amendment confer new power on Congress?
10. Is a *capitation* tax a *direct* tax or an *indirect* tax?

CHAPTER TWO

JUST WHAT IS INCOME FOR TAX PURPOSE?

"What is it that is actually being taxed? Is it people? Is it property? Or is it activities? There cannot be any intelligent conversation about a tax until the actual subject of the tax is known."

Otto Skinner.

Most of us think of income as being whatever comes in to us from our work or investments. Like many words we use in common language, income, also has a legal - meaning and whatever its meaning was in 1913 when the 16th Amendment to the Constitution was ratified; that is what its meaning must remain for tax purposes. We can't change a word's meaning that has a specific import in the Constitution, as that would in effect amend the Constitution.

So let's take a look at what the Supreme Court has stated about the definition of the word "income"

Eisner v. Macomber, 252 U.S. 189, 207, 40 S.Ct. 189, 9 A.L.R. 1570 (1920):

"In order, therefore, that the clauses cited from article 1 of the Constitution may have proper force and effect, save only as modified by the amendment, and that the latter also may have proper effect, it becomes essential to distinguish between what is and what is not 'income,' as the term is there used, and to apply the distinction, as cases arise, according to truth and substance, without regard to form. Congress cannot by any definition it may adopt conclude the matter, since it cannot by legislation alter the Constitution, from which alone it derives its power to legislate, and within whose limitations alone that power can be lawfully exercised.

After examining dictionaries in common use (Bouv. L. D.; Standard Dict.; Webster's Internat. Dict.; Century Dict.), we find little to add to the succinct definition adopted in two cases arising under the Corporation Tax Act of 1909 (Stratton's Independence v. Howbert, <u>231 U.S. 399, 415</u>, 34 S. Sup. Ct. 136, 140 [58 L. Ed. 285]; Doyle v. Mitchell Bros. Co., 247 U.S. 179, 185, 38 S. Sup. Ct. 467, 469 [62 L. Ed. 1054]), <u>'Income may be defined as the gain derived from capital, from labor, or from both combined,' provided it be understood to include profit gained through a sale or conversion of capital assets, to which it was applied in the Doyle Case</u>, 247 U.S. 183, 185 , 38 S. Sup. Ct. 467, 469 (62 L. Ed. 1054)." [emphasis added]

It is interesting to note that <u>income</u> is defined <u>as the gain</u> derived from capital, from labor, or both combined. Now if you consider all you get from your labor to be gain then you must value your labor as worthless. I suspect that your labor already has the value you place on it. To me income is being described in the Eisner Case to be that which comes in as a gain over and above the cost of labor and capital combined. This is what happens in business when you take labor and convert capital to produce a product, which sells for more than the raw cost of labor and capital.

The next thing we will look at is a description of that which is not income where the Eisner Court gives us an example of something that is not income. It is also interesting to note that the court is confirming that direct taxes still have to be apportioned as required by the Constitution before, and apparently after, the 16th Amendment.

"The word 'income' as used in the Amendment does not include a stock dividend since such a dividend is capital and not income and

can be taxed only if the tax is apportioned among the several states..."
Eisner v. Macomber, 252 US 189 (1920)

So is it getting clearer to you just what is and isn't income?
Let's look at some additional cases.

U.S. Supreme Court Merchants' Loan & Trust Co. v. Smietanka, 255 U.S. 509 (1921)

"It is obvious that these decisions in principle rule the case at bar
if the word 'income' has the same (Trust Company vs. Smietanka
255 US 509) meaning as the Income Tax Act of 1913 that it
had in the Corporation Excise Tax Act of 1909, and that it has
the same scope of meaning was in effect decided in Southern
Pacific Co. v. Lowe, 247 U.S. 330, 335, where it was assumed
for the purposes of decision that there was no difference in its
meaning as used in the Act of 1909 and in the Income Tax Act
of 1913. There can be no doubt that the word must be given the
same meaning and content in the Income Tax Acts of 1916 and
1917 that it had in the Act of 1913. When to this we add that in
Eisner v. Macomber, Supra, arising under the Corporation Excise
Tax Act of 1909, with the addition that it should include 'profit
gained through a sale or conversion of capital assets,' there would
seem to be no room to doubt that the word must be given the
same meaning in all of the Income Tax Acts of Congress that was
given to it in the Corporation Excise Tax Act and that what that
meaning is has now become definitely settled by decisions of this
court." [emphasis added]

Doyle v. Mitchell Brothers Co., 247 U.S. 179, 185, 38 S.Ct. 467 (1918)

"Yet it is plain, we think, that by the true intent and meaning
of the act the entire proceeds of a mere conversion of capital
assets were not to be treated as income. Whatever difficulty there
may be about a precise and scientific definition of 'income,' it
imports, as used here, something entirely distinct from principal
or capital either as a subject of taxation or as a measure of the

tax; conveying rather the idea of gain or increase arising from corporate activities. As was said in Stratton's Independence v. Howbert, 231 U.S. 399, 415 , 34 S. Sup. Ct. 136: 'Income may be defined as the gain derived from capital, from labor, or from both combined."

In the Doyle case above the court refers to income (as used in that case) as conveying the idea of gain or increase arising from corporate activities and not the conversion of capital assets (tangible property which can't easily be turned into cash). If that were true then why would we consider the conversion of labor to be income? This case also mentions the idea that income could be either the subject or the measure of the tax; but in both scenarios it would apply to a gain and not a mere conversion. So if the term *income* means gain and meant gain when it was placed in the Constitution under the 16th Amendment, then what does net income mean? Does it mean net gain?

This is what income is: "Income may be defined as the gain derived from capital, from labor or both combined." This is citing Stratton's Independence v. Howbert 231 U.S. 399, 415 34 S. Sup. Ct. 136

So, if your labor is without value then I suspect that all you have come in from it is gain or income. Assuming that, then you have to move to just exactly what is taxable income or taxable gain (more on that later).

Of course corporations are only taxed on their net gain and if they pay you an hourly rate for your labor then they deduct that cost before they calculate income (gain). They deduct your labor cost to them as they would their raw materials cost. Corporations also deduct all of that which they need to exist, every last expense needed to run the business including rent, electricity, phones and stamps. You name it, they can deduct it, before they begin to come up with taxable income, (taxable profit, gain).

Stratton's Independence v. Howbert, <u>231 U.S. 399</u>, **414, 58 L.Ed. 285, 34 Sup.Ct. 136 (1913):**

> "As has been repeatedly remarked, the corporation tax act of 1909 was not intended to be and is not, in any proper sense, an income tax law. This court had decided in the Pollock Case that the income tax law of 1894 amounted in effect to a direct tax upon property, and was invalid because not apportioned according to populations, as prescribed by the Constitution. <u>The act of 1909 avoided this difficulty by imposing not an income tax, but an excise tax upon the conduct of business in a corporate capacity, measuring, however, the amount of tax by the income of the corporation</u>, with certain qualifications prescribed by the act itself. Flint v. Stone Tracy Co. 220 U.S. 107 , 55 L. ed. 389, 31 Sup. Ct. Rep. 342, Ann. Cas. 1912 B, 1312; McCoach v. Minehill & S. H. R. Co. 228 U.S. 295 , 57 L. ed. 842, 33 Sup. Ct. Rep. 419; United States v. Whitridge (decided at this term, 231 U.S. 144 , 58 L. ed. --, 34 Sup. Ct. Rep. 24." [emphasis added]

Here we learn that Congress can lay an <u>excise tax</u> and measure the tax by the <u>amount of income</u>; that, of course, would not require apportionment as it is an indirect, not a direct tax. Why? Because the subject is not income (property) as the subject of the tax is a corporate privilege. Again we also know that the measure of the tax is income and that equals gain, not all receipts.

Bowers v. Kerbaugh-Empire Co., 271 U.S. 170, 174, (1926)

> "Income has been taken to mean the same thing as used in the Corporation Excise Tax Act of 1909 (36 Stat. 112) in the 16th Amendment, and in the various revenue acts subsequently passed."

How was the term "income" used in the Corporation Excise Tax Act of 1909? Was it used to mean profit? More importantly, it was used as the <u>measure</u> of the tax not the <u>subject</u> of the tax in that Act.

U.S. v. Whiteridge, 231 U.S. 144, 34 S.Sup. Ct. 24 (1913)

"As repeatedly pointed out by this court, the corporation tax law of 1909 - enacted, as it was, after Congress had proposed to the legislatures of the several states the adoption of the 16th Amendment to the Constitution, but before the ratification of that Amendment - <u>imposed an excise or privilege tax, and not in any sense a tax upon property or upon income merely as income</u>. It was enacted in view of the decision of this court in Pollock v. Farmers' Loan & T. Co. 157 U.S. 429 , 39 L. ed. 759, 15 Sup. St. Rep. 673, 158 U.S. 601, 39 L. ed. 1108, 15 Sup. Ct. Rep. 912, which held the income tax provisions of a previous law (act of August 27, 1894, 28 Stat. at L. chap. 349, pp. 509, 553, 27 etc. U. S. Comp. Stat. 1901, p. 2260) to be unconstitutional because amounting in effect to a direct tax upon property within the meaning of the Constitution, and because not apportioned in the manner required by that instrument." [emphasis added]

Is it now clear that a tax on the property called income (money) would be a direct tax? However, a tax on a revenue taxable activity (or an excise tax), a tax measured by the income, would be an indirect tax. Any tax called an income tax must either be a tax on a revenue taxable activity, with income being the measure of the tax, or if income is the subject of the tax then it would be a direct tax, and then have to be apportioned. What do we have today with the so-called "Income Tax"? Is it apportioned? Is it a tax on a revenue taxable activity? If so, what activities are classified as such under Income Taxes?

Brushaber v. Union Pacific Railroad Co., 240 U.S. 1, 16-17 (1916)

"The conclusion reached in the Pollack case... recognized the fact that taxation on income was, in its nature, an excise..."

This means a tax on a revenue taxable activity with income being the measure of the tax, not the subject. To hold that the money (income) is not the subject, but rather, the means to measure the tax, makes it fit nicely into an excise tax. To hold it otherwise means to say that the property is the subject of the tax, which would be voided for lack of apportionment. So, the so-called income tax must be a tax on a revenue taxable activity and could be nothing else.

Why do I call it the "so-called income tax"? That is because I learned that term from Otto Skinner, and the tax is "so called" because it is not a tax on income per se (as property). A tax can be called an income tax but that in itself does not tell us what the nature of the tax is. By looking at the statute we should be able to tell if income is the subject of the tax or the subject is some revenue taxable activity.

> **Stapler v. U.S., 21 F.Supp. 737, U.S. Dist. Ct. EDPA (1937)**
> "Income within the meaning of the **16ᵗʰ Amendment** and the **Revenue Act** means, gain ... and in such connection gain means profit ... proceeding from property severed from capital, however invested or employed and coming in, received or drawn by the taxpayer for his separate use, benefit and disposal" [emphasis added]

Income means gain or profit, period. I say, end of subject! You must have gain. It must proceed from the property; if you convert property to capital that is not a gain but a conversion. Income must be a gain.

The Court in **Goodrich v. Edwards, 255 U.S. 527 (1921)** ruled similarly and in 1969, the Court ruled in **Conner v. U.S., 303 F.Supp. 1187**, that:

> "Whatever may constitute income, therefore must have the essential feature of gain to the recipient. This was true when the **16ᵗʰ Amendment** became effective, it was true at the time of **Eisner v. Macomber**, supra, it was true under **sect. 22(a)** of the **Internal Revenue Code** of 1938, and it is likewise true under **sect. 61(a)** of the **I.R.S. Code** of 1954. If there is not gain, there is not income...."

Congress has taxed INCOME and not compensation." [emphasis added]

This case tells us that Congress has taxed INCOME and not compensation. And if, income is gain then what is compensation? Is it value for value?

Edwards v. Keith, 231 F. 111, (1916)
"... one does not derive income by rendering services and charging for them."

The state courts do follow the lead of the U.S. Supreme Court:

"There is a clear distinction between profit and wages or compensation for labor. Compensation for labor cannot be regarded as profit within the meaning of the law." **Oliver v. Halstead, 196 Va. 992, 86 S.E. 2nd 858 (1955)**

"Reasonable compensation for labor or services rendered is not profit." **Lauderdale Cemetery Assoc. v. Matthews, 345 Pa. 239 (1946), 47 A.2d. 277, 280**

If something is not profit and is not gain then it certainly is not income.

So. Pacific v. Lowe, 238 F. 847; (U.S. Dist. Ct. S.D. N.Y. 1917); 247 U.S. 30 (1918)
"... 'income' as used in the statute should be given a meaning so as not to include everything that comes in, the true function of the words 'gains' and 'profits' is to limit the meaning of the word 'income'"

From this I interpret that when it comes to income taxes the words *gains* and *profits* limit the term "income", and that it does not include all that comes in. How do you see it?

Eisner v. Macomber, 252 U.S. 189, 207, 40 S.Ct. 189, 9 A.L.R. 1570 (1920):

"... the definition of income approved by the Court is: 'The gain derived from capital, from labor, or from both combined, provided it be understood to include profits gained through sale or conversion of capital assets.'"

Here the court tells us that the **gain derived from** capital and from labor is **Income**. Not the capital converted to cash, or, the labor converted to cash, but the gain derived from those two things. If you value your labor at zero then all you get for it is gain, but how can you value it at zero when your employer values it at what he gives you for it? Is it worth zero or is it worth what you get for it?

Helvering v. Edison Bros. Stores, 133 F.2d 575 (1943)

"The Treasury Department cannot, by interpretative regulations, make income of that which is not income within the meaning of the revenue acts of Congress, nor can Congress, <u>without appor-</u><u>tionment</u>, tax as income that which is not income within the meaning of the Sixteenth Amendment. Eisner v. Macomber, 252 U.S. 189, 40 S. Ct. 189, 64 L. Ed. 521, 9 A.L.R. 1570; M. E. Blatt Co. v. United States, 305 U.S. 267, 59 S. Ct. 186, 83 L. Ed. 167." [emphasis added]

Do we not understand at this point that income is a gain produced in a revenue taxable activity? It is not the property which comes to us in exchange for our labor or capital, as, for one thing, that is not gain, and for another, it is not the subject of any tax, for if it were it would have to be apportioned. Income is gain and it comes from revenue taxable activities - period!

Southern Pacific Co., v. Lowe, 247 U.S. 330, 335, 38 S.Ct. 540 (1918)

<u>"We must reject in this case, as we have rejected in cases arising</u>

under the Corporation Excise Tax Act of 1909 (Doyle, Collector, v. Mitchell Brothers Co., 247 U.S. 179, 38 Sup. Ct. 467, 62 L. Ed.--), the broad contention submitted on behalf of the government that all receipts—everything that comes in-are income within the proper definition of the term 'gross income,' and that the entire proceeds of a conversion of capital assets, in whatever form and under whatever circumstances accomplished, should be treated as gross income. Certainly the term 'income' has no broader meaning in the 1913 act than in that of 1909 (see Stratton's Independence v. Howbert, 231 U.S. 399, 416, 417 S., 34 Sup. Ct. 136), and for the present purpose we assume there is no difference in its meaning as used in the two acts."[emphasis added]

In this very early case, heard shortly after the sixteenth amendment was passed, the Supreme Court tells us that the contention by the government that all that comes in is to be included in gross income is erroneous. Why are we then led to believe that that is the way it is with personal compensation? That which is not income can never be gross income as well. Income is gain or profit not a conversion of capital or labor.

"There is a clear distinction between 'profit' and 'wages', or a compensation for labor. Compensation for labor (wages) cannot be regarded as profit within the meaning of the law. The word 'profit', as ordinarily used, means the gain made upon any business or investment -- a different thing altogether from the mere compensation for labor."
[Oliver v. Halstead, 86 S.E. Rep 2nd 85e9 (1955)]

This, to me, dispels the notion that our labor is profit. Our labor is an exchange of value for value. How can we see it as anything else?

Butcher's Union v. Crescent City, 111 US 746 (1918)

"… the property which every man has in his own labor, as it is the original foundation of all other property, so it is the most sacred and inviolable. ... to hinder his employing this strength and dexterity in what manner he thinks proper without injury to his neighbor, is a plain violation of this most sacred property."

So whenever we trade value for value is there income? Do we own property in this country? Is our body our property? Is our labor our property? Does our labor have a value?

Penn Mutual Indemnity Co. v. Commissioner, 32 Tax Court page 681:

"The rule of Eisner v. Macomber has been reaffirmed on so many occasions that citation of the cases to this effect would be unnecessarily burdensome. To depart from the rule at this late date would ignore the sound principles upon which that case was decided and would throw into confusion the fundamental income tax structure and law as it has developed in the almost half century which has elapsed since adoption of the 16th amendment. That there cannot be 'income' without a 'gain' accords with the common understanding of the term, a test of construction which is particularly appropriate in our system of self-assessed Federal income tax ... Moreover, that which is not income in fact manifestly cannot be made such by the legislative expedient of calling it income...."

Spreckels Sugar Ref. Co. v. Mclain, 24 SCt 382 (1904):

"the citizen is exempt from taxation unless the same is imposed by clear and unequivocal language."

Is it made clear to us what the subject of the so-called income tax is? Is it made clear to us <u>peasants</u> just what income is? Is it defined in the Internal Revenue Code? Are the income tax laws in this country clear and unequivocal? Do we, as individuals, get to deduct everything we need to exist as the corporations do, before any tax is considered due and owing?

Is the tyranny upon your mind starting to recede? I hope so.

CHAPTER THREE

WHAT IS A TAXPAYER AND HOW DOES ONE BECOME LEGALLY LIABLE FOR AN INTERNAL REVENUE TAX?

"What is it that is actually being taxed? Is it people? Is it property? Or is it activities? There cannot be any intelligent conversation about a tax until the actual subject of the tax is known."

Otto Skinner.

Before we get into the internal revenue definition of *taxpayer*, (one word) let's first cover the phrase *tax payer* (two words). Anyone who pays any kind of tax is considered a *tax payer* or a person who pays taxes. There is a significant difference between taxpayer and *tax payer*. If someone asked you if you are a *tax payer* that is quite different than if they asked you if you were a *taxpayer*. There is a legal significance between the two concepts.

Taxpayer is a term defined in the Internal Revenue Code whereas the Code does not make any reference to a tax payer. You, of course, see that one term is one word and the other is two words. Let's look at the Internal Revenue Code to see how they define "taxpayer" – one word.

Title 26

> **Section 7701(a)(14) defines the term "taxpayer" to mean** "any person **subject to** any internal **revenue tax".** [emphasis added]
>
> **Section 1313(b) defines the "taxpayer" to mean "any** person **subject to a tax under the applicable revenue law".** [emphasis added]

The United States Court of Appeals for the Fifth Circuit tells us that:

> We see no distinction between the phrases "**liable for** such tax" and **subject to** a tax. Houston Street Corp. VCJ.R., 84 F.2d 821, at 822($_{5th}$ Cir. 1936). [emphasis added]

So, from now on, please train your mind to the difference between <u>tax payer</u> and <u>taxpayer</u>. Almost all of us are <u>tax payers</u> but not that many of us are <u>taxpayers</u>.

Now that we have some familiarity with the different classes, categories and types of taxes such as indirect, direct, impost, excises, duties and tariffs, to name a few, how do you suppose any of us become liable for, or subject to, any tax imposed in the Internal Revenue Code? Yes, that's right, there must be a law imposing the obligation on us. Do you disagree with this?

We will shortly read some tax impositions in the Internal Revenue Code. I pulled these examples randomly. Let's look at these different taxes, with one objective in mind, 'who is it that is being made liable for (subject to) the tax'? That is, who is becoming a taxpayer by the imposition of <u>liability</u>?

TITLE 26 - INTERNAL REVENUE CODE
SUBTITLE D - MISCELLANEOUS EXCISE TAXES
CHAPTER 32 - MANUFACTURERS EXCISE TAXES
SUBCHAPTER A - AUTOMOTIVE AND RELATED ITEMS
PART I - GAS GUZZLERS

Section 4064. Gas-guzzler tax

(a) Imposition of tax

> There is hereby imposed on the sale by the manufacturer of each automobile a tax determined in accordance with the following table:

Can you tell who is made liable for the tax? Personally, it is not clear to me who is it that is being made liable for (subject to) the tax. I think we are left to assume that the manufacturer is the one liable? Let's look at another example.

TITLE 26 - INTERNAL REVENUE CODE
SUBTITLE E - ALCOHOL, TOBACCO, AND CERTAIN OTHER EXCISE TAXES
CHAPTER 51 - DISTILLED SPIRITS, WINES, AND BEER
SUBCHAPTER A. GALLONAGE AND OCCUPATIONAL TAXES
SUBPART A - DISTILLED SPIRITS

Section 5001.Imposition, rate, and attachment of tax
   (a) Rate of tax
      (1) General
> There is hereby imposed on all distilled spirits produced in or imported into the United States a tax at the rate of $13.50 on each proof gallon and a proportionate tax at the like rate on all fractional parts of a proof gallon.

Section 5005. Persons liable for tax
   (a) General
> The distiller or importer of distilled spirits shall be liable for the taxes imposed thereon by section 5001(a)(1).

Who is it that's being made liable, that is, **subject** to the tax? It is quite clear that the <u>distiller or importer</u> is the <u>person being made liable</u> and thusly, the one <u>becoming a "taxpayer"</u> at this point; that is, someone who is made subject to an internal revenue tax. (see definitions above)

Look at the next section with the same object in mind, that is, just who it is that is being made liable for the tax. In other words, who is <u>becoming a taxpayer</u> at this point?

SUBPART C - WINES

Section 5041. Imposition and rate of tax

(a) Imposition

There is hereby imposed on all wines (including imitation, substandard, or artificial wine, and compounds sold as wine) having not in excess of 24 percent of alcohol by volume, in bond in, produced in, or imported into, the United States, taxes at the rates shown in subsection

At this point it is not possible to tell who is being made into a taxpayer. We need the liability section that relates to the imposition. We find that in section 5043.

Section 5043. Collection of taxes on wines

(a) Persons liable for payment

The taxes on wine provided for in this subpart shall be paid—

(1) Bonded wine cellars

In the case of wines removed from any bonded wine cellar, <u>by the proprietor</u> of such bonded wine cellar; except that—

(A) in the case of any transfer of wine in bond as authorized under the provisions of section 5362 (b), the <u>liability for payment of the tax shall become the</u> <u>liability of the transferee</u> from the time of removal of the wine from the transferor's premises, and the transferor shall thereupon be relieved of such liability; and

(B) in the case of any <u>wine withdrawn by a person</u> other than such proprietor without payment of tax as authorized under the provisions of section 5362

(c), the <u>liability for payment of the tax shall become the liability of such person</u> from the time of the removal of the wine from the bonded wine cellar, and such proprietor shall thereupon be relieved of such liability.

(2) Foreign wine

In the case of foreign wines which are not transferred to a bonded wine cellar free of tax under section 5364, <u>by the importer thereof.</u>

(3) Other wines

Immediately, in the case of any wine produced, imported, received, removed, or possessed otherwise than as authorized by law, by any person producing, importing, receiving, removing, or possessing such wine; and <u>all such persons shall be jointly and severally liable</u> for such tax with each other as well as with any proprietor, transferee, or importer who may be liable for the tax under this subsection. [emphasis added]

These impositions of tax are making it clear just who is liable or subject to the tax. These are the people who are becoming taxpayers (someone subject to or liable for an internal revenue tax). As we read these sections we find the tax imposed and then we find just who is being made liable. Here is another example.

TITLE 26 - INTERNAL REVENUE CODE
SUBTITLE B - ESTATE AND GIFT TAXES
CHAPTER 11 - ESTATE TAX
SUBCHAPTER A - ESTATES OF CITIZENS OR RESIDENTS
PART I - TAX IMPOSED

Section 2001. Imposition and rate of tax
  (a) Imposition
  A tax is hereby imposed on the transfer of the taxable estate of every decedent who is a citizen or resident of the United States. Computation of tax The tax imposed by this section shall be the amount equal to the...

Section 2002. Liability for payment
  The executor shall pay the tax imposed by this chapter.

Again, is someone being made liable for the tax in sec 2002? Is someone being made into a taxpayer with this code section? Is it clear that the code has to impose a duty or a liability on someone before they become a taxpayer?

TITLE 26 - INTERNAL REVENUE CODE
SUBTITLE D - MISCELLANEOUS EXCISE TAXES
CHAPTER 31 - RETAIL EXCISE TAXES
SUBCHAPTER A - LUXURY PASSENGER AUTOMOBILES

Section 4001. Imposition of tax
  (a) Imposition of tax
    (1) In general
       There is hereby imposed on the 1st retail sale of any passenger vehicle a tax equal to 10 percent of the price for which so sold to the extent such price exceeds the applicable amount.

(2) Applicable amount
(A) In general
Except as provided in subparagraphs (B) and (C), the applicable amount is $30,000.

Are you able to determine who it is that is being made liable for the tax imposed in Section 4001? Maybe you need the liability section to find that out. Let's look at it.

Section 4002. 1st retail sale; uses, etc. treated as sales; determination of price

(a) 1st retail sale
For purposes of this subchapter, the term "1st retail sale" means the 1st sale, for a purpose other than resale, after manufacture, production, or importation.

(b) Use treated as sale
(1) In general
If any person uses a passenger vehicle (including any use after importation) before the 1st retail sale of such vehicle, then such person shall be liable for tax under this subchapter in the same manner as if such vehicle were sold at retail by him.

Now can you find the taxpayer (person made liable for or subject to the tax)? Let's look at another section in the code.

TITLE 26 - INTERNAL REVENUE CODE
SUBTITLE D - MISCELLANEOUS EXCISE TAXES
CHAPTER 35 – ON WAGERING
SUBCHAPTER A – TAX ON WAGERS

Section 4401. Imposition of tax
(a) Wagers
(1) State authorized wagers

There shall be imposed on any wager authorized under the law of the State in which accepted an excise tax equal to 0.25 percent of the amount of such wager.

(2) Unauthorized wagers

There shall be imposed on any wager not described in paragraph (1) an excise tax equal to 2 percent of the amount of such wager.

(c) Persons liable for tax

<u>Each person who is engaged</u> in the business of accepting wagers <u>shall be liable </u>for and shall pay the tax under this subchapter on all wagers placed and shall pay the tax under this subchapter on all wagers placed in such pool or lottery. Any person required to register under section 4412 who receives wagers for or on behalf of another person without having registered under section 4412 the name and place of residence of such other person shall be liable for and shall pay the tax under this subchapter on all such wagers received by him.

Are you finding that it is easier for you to determine who is made liable for any tax imposed by this Title (the Internal Revenue Code)?

Here is the one (Income Tax) you have been waiting for - right? When reading, look for the statements you are used to looking for. That is, just who is being made liable for a tax. Or are you supposed to assume someone is being made liable for that tax?

TITLE 26 - INTERNAL REVENUE CODE
SUBTITLE A - INCOME TAXES
CHAPTER 1 - NORMAL TAXES AND SURTAXES
SUBCHAPTER A - DETERMINATION OF TAX LIABILITY
PART I - TAX ON INDIVIDUALS

Section 1. Tax imposed

(a) Married individuals filing joint returns and surviving spouses

There is hereby imposed on the taxable income of—

> **(1)** every married individual (as defined in section 7703) who makes a single return jointly with his spouse under section 6013, and

> **(2)** every surviving spouse (as defined in section 2 (a)), a tax determined in accordance with the following table:

(b) Heads of households

There is hereby imposed on the taxable income of every head of a household (as defined in section 2 (b)) a tax determined in accordance with the following table:

(c) Unmarried individuals (other than surviving spouses and heads of households)

There is hereby imposed on the taxable income of every individual (other than a surviving spouse as defined in section 2 (a) or the head of a household as defined in section 2 (b)) who is not a married individual (as defined in section 7703) a tax determined in accordance with the following table:

(d) Married individuals filing separate returns

There is hereby imposed on the taxable income of every married individual (as defined in section 7703) who does not make a single return jointly with his spouse under section 6013, a tax determined in accordance with the following table:

The strange thing about this, so called, income tax is that you can't find anywhere in the code where someone is being made liable for it. So, unlike the other impositions in the code, we are unable to quickly determine the subject of the <u>so</u> <u>called</u> <u>income</u> <u>tax</u> and the person made liable.

Another strange thing about the so called income tax is that it appears to be imposed on something called <u>taxable</u> <u>income</u>. Do you remember what <u>taxable</u> <u>income</u> is?

Even at that, it appears that all gain is not taxable or all income is not taxable. What is taxable income? Do you have any, or at this point can you tell if you have any? Do you have any gain that is taxable?

This book is written, partially, to help create an understanding that the legal term "taxpayer" clearly means someone who is subject to an internal revenue tax and that to become a taxpayer there must be a code section that makes you subject to or liable for an internal revenue tax.

I can't find the section that makes anyone liable or subject to an income tax and until someone shows me, I remain a non-taxpayer; that is, someone who is not liable for an internal revenue tax. The Internal Revenue Code is replete with references to the term "taxpayer" and clearly all the liability and penalties in the code are regarding someone who is subject to the code.

The next chapter will deal with the actual subject of different taxes. The actual "subject" of a tax is paramount to determining if the tax is direct or indirect and for you to be able to determine if you are a person made liable for that subject. Hopefully we will find out what the "subject" of the so called income tax is (Or maybe not, because it just might not exist).

CHAPTER FOUR

WHAT IS THE SUBJECT OF THE SO CALLED INCOME TAX?

To know if you have an income tax liability it is paramount to know just what the subject of the income tax is. Is it *people, property* or some sort of *activity* that is being taxed? Why is it impossible to get that question answered by anyone at the IRS? If the tax is on people or property then that would make the tax a direct tax which, if you will recall, **MUST** be apportioned. If the tax is on some sort of activity then it would be an indirect tax and not subject to the rule of apportionment.

Here is a little refresher on direct taxes.

DIRECT, a. [L., to make straight. See Right.]: (Webster 1828)

Direct tax, is a tax assess on real estate, as houses and lands.

Article 1; Section 9., Paragraph 4

No Capitation, or other direct, Tax shall be laid, unless in Proportion to the Census or Enumeration herein before directed to be taken.

Stanton v. Baltic Mining (240 U.S. 103), 1916:

"..by the previous ruling it was settled that the provisions of the Sixteenth Amendment <u>conferred no new power of taxation</u> but simply prohibited the previous complete and plenary power of income taxation possessed by Congress from the beginning from being taken out of the category of indirect taxation to which it inherently belonged and being placed in the category of direct taxation. [emphasis added]

With just this information we know two very important things. One, that an income tax is an indirect tax and two, it therefore must not be a tax on property, as property taxes are direct. That leaves us with it having to be a tax on an activity.

We will now look at several taxes imposed by the code <u>for the sole purpose of trying to determine just what the "subject" of the tax is</u>. In the last chapter we looked at this imposition with the idea of trying to find out who was liable.

TITLE 26 - INTERNAL REVENUE CODE
SUBTITLE D - MISCELLANEOUS EXCISE TAXES
CHAPTER 32 - MANUFACTURERS EXCISE TAXES
SUBCHAPTER A - AUTOMOTIVE AND RELATED ITEMS
PART I - GAS GUZZLERS

Section 4064. Gas guzzler tax
  (a) **Imposition of tax**
      There is hereby imposed <u>on the sale </u>by the manufacturer of each automobile a tax determined in accordance with the following table: [emphasis added]

Is this a tax imposed on an activity, some sort of property, or a person? Obviously it is a person that becomes liable for taxes but if they are the subject of the tax then the tax would be a direct tax. A head tax or poll tax would make a person the subject but that is different than being the one made liable. Is the tax, imposed above, a direct tax or an indirect tax? I think it is quite clear that the tax is on "the sale" which is an activity. So that would be the subject of the tax; that is, the activity of the sale.

Let's look at another example, just to try to determine what the subject of the tax is.

TITLE 26 - INTERNAL REVENUE CODE
SUBTITLE E - ALCOHOL, TOBACCO, AND CERTAIN
OTHER EXCISE TAXES CHAPTER 51 - DISTILLED
SPIRITS, WINES, AND BEER

Subchapter A. Gallonage And Occupational Taxes

SUBPART A - DISTILLED SPIRITS

Section 5001. Imposition, rate, and attachment of tax
   (a) Rate of tax
      (1) General
      There is hereby imposed on all distilled spirits produced in or imported into the United States a tax at the rate of $13.50 on each proof gallon and a proportionate tax at the like rate on all fractional parts of a proof gallon.

Can you see that the subject of the tax is "production" and/or "importation" of distilled spirits and not the spirits themselves? Are you able to see that the spirits themselves are not the subject of the tax? What if Congress actually made distilled spirits the subject of a tax? Would they then have to apportion the tax as being a direct tax? You know, split the tax bill up among the states according to the population percentage of each state. The main objective here is that you are able to tell what the subject of the tax is and do it with certainty.

Once again, read the next section with the idea in mind that you are looking for the subject of the tax.

SUBPART C - WINES

Section 5041. Imposition and rate of tax imposition

There is hereby imposed <u>on all wines</u> (including imitation, substandard, or artificial wine, and compounds sold as wine) having not in excess of 24 percent of alcohol by volume, <u>in bond in</u>, <u>produced in</u>, or <u>imported into</u>, the United States, taxes at the rates shown in subsection

Is it a tax on an activity, persons or property? Is wine (property) the subject of the tax or is "in bond in, produced in, or imported into" the subject of the tax? Can you see it is not the property, wine, that is the subject of the tax, but, rather, certain activities that the property (wine) becomes involved in which are the subject of the tax? There may be confusion here because this section starts off with the phrase "imposed on all wine", just as when we come across the income tax and it says, imposed on the "taxable income", our mind wants to think that all wines are the subject of the tax as it thinks taxable income is the subject regarding the income tax. So, it is the word "on" that leads us to a false conclusion. It would be much easier for us if the wording was, *"There is hereby imposed on the bonding, importation into, or production of all wines in the United States.* The proper interpretation of "on all wines" would be, "in regards to" all wines or "regarding" all wines.

We can also know that wine is not the subject of the tax because, if the property, wine, was the subject, then the tax would have to be apportioned. Prevailing logic shows us that the subject of this tax is certain activities Congress has deemed taxable.

Again let's look for the subject in the next imposition of taxes.

TITLE 26 - INTERNAL REVENUE CODE
SUBTITLE B - ESTATE AND GIFT TAXES
CHAPTER 11 - ESTATE TAX
SUBCHAPTER A ESTATES OF CITIZENS OR RESDENTS
PART I - TAX IMPOSED

Section 2001. Imposition and rate of tax

(a) Imposition

A tax is hereby <u>imposed on the transfer</u> of the <u>taxable estate</u> of every decedent who is a citizen or resident of the United States. [emphasis added]

(b) Computation of tax

The tax imposed by this section shall be the amount equal to the...

What do you find the subject of the above tax to be: property, activity, or people? I find that it is on "the transfer" of something called a taxable estate. At this point we don't know what a taxable estate is. It is the transfer that creates the imposition.

TITLE 26 - INTERNAL REVENUE CODE
SUBTITLE D - MISCELLANEOUS EXCISE TAXES
CHAPTER 31 - RETAIL EXCISE TAXES
SUBCHAPTER A - LUXURY PASSENGER AUTOMOBILES

Section 4001. Imposition of tax

(a) Imposition of tax

(1) In general

There is hereby <u>imposed on the 1st retail sale</u> of any passenger vehicle a tax equal to 10 percent of the price for which so sold to the extent such price exceeds the applicable amount. [emphasis added]

(2) Applicable amount

    (A) In general

        Except as provided in subparagraphs (B) and (C), the applicable amount is $30,000.

        Answer the same question here. Is this a direct or indirect tax and is it on an activity, people or property? If this is a tax on an activity as opposed to property, then what would that activity be?

TITLE 26 - INTERNAL REVENUE CODE
SUBTITLE D - MISCELLANEOUS EXCISE TAXES
CHAPTER 35 – ON WAGERING
SUBCHAPTER A – TAX ON WAGERS

Section 4401. Imposition of tax

    (a) Wagers

        (1) State authorized wagers

            There shall be imposed <u>on any wager authorized under</u> the law of the State in which accepted an excise tax equal to 0.25 percent of the amount of such wager. [emphasis added]

        (2) Unauthorized wagers

            There shall be <u>imposed on any wager</u> not described in paragraph (1) an excise tax equal to 2 percent of the amount of such wager. [emphasis added]

Is this a direct or indirect tax and is it on an activity, people or property? If this is a tax on an activity as opposed to property then what would that activity be?

Here is the big daddy of them all. This small subsection applies to married individuals. The wording in the other classifications is quite similar. Please read this with the idea in mind of trying to find out what the subject of the tax is.

TITLE 26 - INTERNAL REVENUE CODE
SUBTITLE A - INCOME TAXES
CHAPTER 1 - NORMAL TAXES AND SURTAXES
SUBCHAPTER A - DETERMINATION OF TAX LIABILITY
PART I - TAX ON INDIVIDUALS

Section 1. Tax imposed

    (a) Married individuals filing joint returns and surviving spouses

There is hereby <u>imposed on the taxable</u> income of— (1) every married individual (as defined in section 7703) who makes a single return jointly with his spouse under section 6013, and (2) every surviving spouse (as defined in section 2 (a)), a tax determined in accordance with the following table: [emphasis added]

    (b) Heads of households

There is hereby <u>imposed on the taxable income</u> of every head of a household (as defined in section 2 (b)) a tax determined in accordance with the following table: [emphasis added]

    (c) Unmarried individuals (other than surviving spouses and heads of households)

There is hereby <u>imposed on the taxable</u> income of every individual (other than a surviving spouse as defined in section 2 (a) or the head of a household as defined in section 2 (b)) who is not a married individual (as defined in section 7703) a tax determined in accordance with the following table: [emphasis added]

    (d) Married individuals filing separate returns

There is hereby <u>imposed on the taxable income</u> of every married individual (as defined in section 7703) who does not make a single return jointly with his spouse under section

6013, a tax determined in accordance with the following
table: [emphasis added]

Let's do the same drill. Is this tax imposed on property, people or an
activity? Is it a direct or indirect tax? At first glance we might think this
is some kind of tax on property (taxable income) but that would mean
that it would be a direct tax. As you will recall, direct taxes are laid on
people and property, and indirect taxes are imposed on excises and the
like. Remember the imposition of a tax on all wines? It was not a tax on
the wines themselves, which would be a property tax or a direct tax, but
instead it was a tax on the importation, among other things, of the wine.
It was a tax on what Congress deemed a taxable activity, but in no way a
tax on the property. So it is with a tax on taxable income. The tax would
be <u>regarding</u> taxable income but the <u>subject</u> of the tax would be some
revenue taxable activity. Just what that activity might be is conveniently
(?) missing.

Notice 1 (a) above states; "There is hereby <u>imposed on the taxable</u>
income of— (1) every married individual (as defined in section 7703)
<u>who makes a single return </u>jointly with his spouse under section 6013,
and"

Notice that the tax is being imposed on persons filing returns who
have taxable income. If one files a return saying that they owe money
then I suppose we can't object to the government imposing a tax on that
activity. What happens if you don't file a return? Where is the income
tax imposed? Another way of asking the question is (since this section
imposes a duty on people who file a return) just where in the code do
they impose a tax on someone who does not file a return? I can't find it.
Don't you agree that a tax imposition should be clear? Is it clear that you
are being made a taxpayer under this section? Just where is the liability
imposed?

To me it is quite clear that this is not a direct tax on some sort of
property (known as income) but instead, it would have to be an excise tax
on some revenue taxable activity, and that the measure of the tax would
be found in the income. The question is, just what activity would that

be? Is the activity you do for a living named as a revenue taxable activity in the Internal Revenue Code? I know it is not a direct tax because I know all direct taxes must be apportioned among the states, and that the U. S. Government is not imposing any direct tax currently.

If the Internal Revenue code does not make you liable for an income tax than how do you become liable for the tax, or become a taxpayer? Have you ever signed a 1040 form? If you have, by your signature you are declaring, under the penalty of perjury, that you are a taxpayer or someone subject to an internal revenue tax. Has anyone sent a 1099 to the IRS regarding you? When they do that, are they not reporting that you are a "taxpayer," and that you had taxable income? Have you ever signed any other forms from the IRS that state you are a taxpayer? If any of the above does apply to you, and I suppose that some do that might make you a "taxpayer" in the eyes of the government. However, I can't find where Congress made you one.

To me, it is quite clear that this is not a direct tax on some sort of property known as income, but, instead, it would have to be an excise tax on some revenue taxable activity, and that the measure of the tax would be found in the income. The question is just what activity would that be? Is the activity you do for a living, named as a revenue taxable activity in the Internal Revenue Code?

Do you feel any tyranny lifting from your mind yet?

CHAPTER FIVE

HOW DID YOUR STATUS OF BEING CLASSIFIED AS A TAXPAYER BEGIN AND WHAT CAN YOU DO TO END IT?

Do you remember the first job you had in which you filled out a W4 form? Do you remember what it said on it? Here is what it likely said: "**Purpose**. Complete Form W-4 so that your employer can withhold the correct federal income tax from your pay." You and your employer <u>assumed</u> that you were subject to an income tax.

Who should have federal income tax withheld from their pay, a taxpayer or a non-taxpayer? Are you telling the government, by filling out this form that you are a taxpayer? Were you lead to believe that this form was mandatory by your employer?

Here is what the Code of Federal Regulations says regarding these agreements. The Code of Federal Regulations relate to the U. S. Codes passed by Congress. They are the implementing regulations.

[Code of Federal Regulations]
[Title 26, Volume 15]
[Revised as of January 1, 2007]
From the U.S. Government Printing Office via GPO Access
[CITE: 26CFR31.3402(p)-1]
[Page 262-263]

TITLE 26--INTERNAL REVENUE
CHAPTER I--INTERNAL REVENUE SERVICE,
DEPARTMENT OF THE TREASURY
PART 31_EMPLOYMENT TAXES AND COLLECTION OF
INCOME TAX AT SOURCE--Table

Subpart E Collection of Income Tax at Source

Sec. 31.3402(p)-1 Voluntary withholding agreements.

(a) In general. An employee and his employer <u>may enter into an</u> <u>agreement</u> under section 3402(b) to provide for the with-holding of income tax upon payments of amounts described in paragraph (b)(1) of Sec. 31.3401(a)-3, made after December 31, 1970. An agreement may be entered into under this section only with respect to amounts which are includible in the gross income of the employee under section 61, and must be applicable to all such amounts paid by the employer to the employee. The amount to be withheld pursuant to an agreement under section 3402(p) shall [emphasis added]

This regulation states that the withholding agreements are voluntary and that the agreement is for withholding income tax. So logic dictates that when you enter into such agreements, you are stating that you <u>are</u> **liable for** income taxes, that is, are **subject to** them. Ah, magic! You told the government that you are a taxpayer subject to the Internal Revenue Code. (You know, it is a lot easier for them when you do that. As for me, they were never able to demonstrate a code section that made me liable.) I know that employers think the form is mandatory, and that they think social security taxes are mandatory as well.

So, each and every payday, after the first one, you and your employer just kept going with this arrangement; with the two of you telling the government that you were a taxpayer. Interesting, right? Of course it is another matter trying to demonstrate that this is voluntary to your employer. Assumptions and presumptions can be mighty powerful. Employers today assume and presume quite a bit - as do we.

Then, on or before April 15th, what did you do? You filed a Form 1040 (a U.S. Individual Income Tax Return) telling the government that you had income (gain) and that you were a "taxpayer", and how much in taxes you actually owed. You even furnished your Taxpayer ID Number - your social security number. You also signed this form under the penalty of perjury. Now do you know why they treat you like a taxpayer? You told them you were one and you did so under the penalties of perjury. Of course they are going to apply all the rules, to you. You have told them this for years and years. Most of you have said, 'I am subject to this involuntary servitude', so many times and now you expect them to let you go easily?

I counted 22 questions on this form 1040 asking if you had a certain kind of income. I don't want to count how many references are made to taxable income and gross income. When looking at this form, try and remember that taxable income is not the subject of a tax as that would require **apportionment**; so then the question is, what taxable activity were you engaged in to have income?

What's the bottom line? You are telling the government that you are a taxpayer when you complete these forms. (I guess you are now wondering, 'how can I escape from this trap'?)

Let's look at the tax called the Social Security Tax in Internal Revenue Code 3101(a), and 3111(a) which are imposition statutes for the (so-called Social Security) FICA tax -- section 3101(a) applying to employees and 3111(a) to employers, respectively.

Sec. 3101. Rate of Tax.

(a) Old-Age, survivors, and disability Insurance. In addition to other taxes, there ***is hereby imposed on the income*** of every individual a tax equal to the following percentages of the wages (as defined in section 3121(a))received by him with respect to employment (as defined in section 3121(b)) – [emphasis added]

Sec. 3111. Rate of Tax.

(a) Old-age, survivors, and disability insurance. In addition to other taxes, there *is hereby imposed on every employer an excise tax*, with respect to having individuals in his employ, equal to the following percentages of the wages (as defined in section 3121(a)) paid by him with respect to employment (as defined In section 3121(b)) –[emphasis added]

Notice how section 3101 (a) states the tax is imposed **on the income** and section 3111 (a) that an excise tax is being imposed. Why do you suppose that section 3101 (a) does not say a tax is imposed on the excise of working? The reason is because an *excise tax* may not be imposed on a *right* - and you certainly have a *right* to labor to sustain your life. If a *right* could be taxed how could it be a *right*? Is it a *right* to live and to do lawful activities to sustain that right?

Besides all of that, did you get paid for the value of your labor or did you receive a '*gain*' out of the exchange of your labor (you know… cheat your employer)? I suppose if he pays you 20 dollars an hour and you only give '10 dollars of value' back in labor, then you just might have income (*gain*).

Another interesting point out of these two code sections is, one imposition is obviously *indirect* (excise tax on employers) and the other, the tax on employees, is vague. Are we to assume the tax on the employee is a *direct tax* while the tax on the employer is an *indirect* one?

Now for the hard part, how does one get out from underneath this tyranny? If you work for someone, frankly, I have heard of only a very few cases in which the employer has let employees out of the noose. I don't know of anyone, nor do I have any data readily accessible, to tell you how to deal with stopping the withholding of income taxes and social security taxes, even if you don't owe them. I suppose the employer can claim that they have to withhold and that if you don't like it then you don't have to work there. I even suppose that some sharp lawyer who really knows this subject might be able to get somewhere with that issue, but I don't know where you can find one at the present time.

So where do you go from there? How about becoming self employed?

Instead of telling you what to do, I will tell you what I wouldn't do, and what I have done. You will have to take full responsibility for whatever choices you make. Once I found out that I was not subject to an Income Tax, or for that matter any Internal Revenue tax, I immediately let the IRS know of my newly discovered status of being a **non**-*taxpayer* all these years. I sent them an affidavit affirming my status as a 'non-taxpayer' and letting them know that in the past I had been misinformed and had signed IRS forms and filed tax returns in error. I also sent in a letter rescinding my social security number. I told them I had signed the form applying for a social security number by mistake. I told them it was an invalid contract as I was a minor at the time of signing up for social security. There is plenty of information out there on the net, and otherwise, to help you do all of this.

So 'is that all there is to it', you ask? I wish that was all. This subject is incredibly complex and compounded, and there is a ton of information, misinformation, and totally false information, as well, to sift through. But if you want to be free of this tyranny, you have to dedicate yourself to study, study, and more study. What I did was study everything I could find on this subject, including large parts of the Internal Revenue Code and several court cases. And because the subject is so complicated, I made myself take a 'critical viewpoint' of everything I read. When someone was stating *an **opinion***, I was quick to note that that was all it was, and not a fact. The only opinions I took for fact were those made by the Supreme Court. Letting common sense rule the day was a very vital part of my education on this subject. Another one was, to not assume anything. I became very insistent of 'show me the law!' I would never ever assume I was a "taxpayer" or had "gross income" or had to 'file a return'. I especially insisted that the government had to prove to me that Title 26 of the U. S. Codes applied to me, and, consequently, the U. S. District Court, regarding any Title 26 action.

The intent of this booklet is to help 'awaken you', and is designed with the purpose in mind of being inexpensive and eye opening without putting you to sleep. I recommend that you read all three books written on this subject by Otto Skinner. They are:

The Biggest "Tax Loophole" of All

"Provides the clearest and best explanation of the so-called "income" tax and the Sixteenth Amendment available to Americans today. This is the most comprehensive of the books covering every aspect of the "Income" tax including Supreme Court decisions as far back as 1796 and as current as today."

The Best Kept Secret, "Taxpayer" v. Non-taxpayer

"Was originally written in 1986 and updated in 1996, with emphasis on the fact that the right to receive earnings or income is a right that cannot be taxed for revenue purposes."

If You Are the Defendant

"Was originally written in 1989 and updated in 1996, with emphasis on defending one's self against alleged violations of the revenue laws."

These books are loaded with valuable information. What I found most intriguing regarding these books is that Otto Skinner did not stuff the books with his opinions nor did he put forth any arguments trying to prove why we don't have to pay an income tax. I have read dozens of arguments from people exerting that they don't have to pay an income tax for one reason or another. Instead of putting the 'burden of proof' on the government to prove just where, if at all, in the Internal Revenue code that they were made subject to an income tax, they, instead, wanted to demonstrate *why they did not have to pay an income tax.* Many of them were all puffed up and very enamored with themselves, feeling that they were the one who discovered why the so called income tax didn't apply to people like them. Otto's method was just the opposite. His was the Socratic method of asking questions. Questions the government would not, or could not, answer. Such as... 'what is **the subject of** the so called income tax'?

I personally have gained some knowledge from some of the authors of the "prove the negative" theories (instead of putting the burden of proof on the government). Otto Skinner holds these people in a less than favorable light. He told me that I should not give these people the benefit of the doubt. His thinking was that they know that they are peddling snake oil. He thought many of the authors of these books were simply profiting falsely (charlatans) from people who were trying to be free of the chains of slavery that the IRS puts us under. These are my words but his sentiments. I must admit it is dangerous, in my opinion, to read some of these experts who engage in an approach that is all about trying to prove why you're not subject to an income tax. Unless you have a discerning mind and can easily recognize opinion from fact you should just stick with Otto's books.

If you want to get out from the yoke of this tyranny, hard work is the only way out. It is not for the indolent, for if you go to battle with these tyrants less than fully prepared, you will probably lose. And many do lose when prepared with the wrong arguments. When studying, study the cases that were wins and the ones that were losses, and cull out for yourself the things you think caused the wins and losses. You may say I don't know if all of this is worth it. Maybe it is, maybe it isn't, but freedom sometimes takes a ton of effort.

Silence is a good policy; I never talk to a tyrant unless I can record it. I make it a practice not to answer questions verbally as that can only get you in trouble as well. Written correspondence will provide you a record of what you have asked and what they have failed to answer. I would not make any assumptions in any correspondence, however, if you have an opinion that you are not a "taxpayer", then you should make that known.

I would never allow anyone to call me a 'tax protestor', either, as I don't protest any tax here. I simply deny owing an income tax or being subject to one. That condition is hardly a tax protester or tax resistor. There is no law that requires someone to pay a tax they do not owe. In fact the law protects us from false or fraudulent tax notices.

What does a person do once they know that they are not a taxpayer but are faced with the new dilemma of being asked to sign forms, under the penalty of perjury, that they are a taxpayer? If you are a person of ethics and integrity can you lie and say you are a taxpayer when you know you're not? Do you lie, as most people who think they are taxpayers lie through their teeth when they are filling out those tax forms? I guess the only honest ones are the ones who know they are not taxpayers and consequently don't fill out IRS forms.

CHAPTER SIX

WHAT DOES THE IRS HAVE TO DO TO ASSESS & COLLECT TAXES IF I DON'T FILE?

Here is where we start to find out what the government has to do to assess income taxes if you don't self-assess. Please notice a key phrase in this section, "imposed by this title". The tax has to be first imposed by this title before the Secretary can do anything in regards to assessments. So just where is the so - called income tax imposed? If it is not imposed - and, specifically imposed on your activities - then how could the Secretary assess it?

TITLE 26
SUBTITLE F
CHAPTER 63
SUBCHAPER A

Section 6201. Assessment authority
  (a) **Authority of Secretary**

      The Secretary is authorized and required to make the inquiries, determinations, and assessments of all taxes (including interest, additional amounts, additions to the tax, and assessable penalties) imposed by this title, or accruing under any former internal revenue law, which have not been duly paid by stamp at the time and in the manner provided by law. Such authority shall extend to and include the following:

(1) Taxes shown on return
The Secretary shall assess all taxes determined by the taxpayer or by the Secretary as to which returns or lists are made under this title.

It is easy for the Secretary to assess taxes from a return you make as you flatly state that you are subject to a tax and you state the amount of tax you should be paying. It is not so easy for the Secretary to assess a tax if you give him nothing to assess.

Section 6203. Method of assessment

The assessment shall be made by recording the liability of the taxpayer in the office of the Secretary in accordance with rules or regulations prescribed by the Secretary. Upon request of the taxpayer, the Secretary shall furnish the taxpayer a copy of the record of the assessment.

Notice the phrase "liability of the taxpayer". How does one become a "**taxpayer**" in regards to an internal revenue tax? They must be made *liable for* or *subject to* an Internal Revenue tax. Only taxpayers get assessed.

The Internal Revenue Code defines "taxpayer" in **Section 7701 (a) (14)** to mean "any person subject to any internal revenue tax". **Section 1313(b)** defines "taxpayer" to mean "any person subject to a tax under the applicable revenue law".

Where is the law, the section in the IR code, (if there is any), that imposes a duty on you? What is the subject of that tax? Is *it people, property* or some *revenue taxable activity*? Since we know that when we tax *people* and *property*, that tax is a Direct tax, and Direct taxes must be apportioned, therefore, if there is an income tax it must be imposed on some '*activity*' as there is no tax that has been **apportioned** in the U.S.

Is it clear that the Secretary can only assess a tax on someone who is <u>subject to</u> an internal revenue tax? If he, or she, was to assess a tax on you, would you not want to know just where that tax obligation was imposed on you, and just what *activity* you were doing that was making you subject to the tax?

Personally, I don't think the Secretary will assess any tax that is <u>not</u> imposed on you; so if you get something called a 'notice of tax deficiency' it might be a good idea to ask for a copy of the 'record of assessment'. Don't settle for a computer printout that indicates there was an assessment, but, instead insist on a copy of the actual assessment. I don't think the IRS will be able to produce one as it makes no sense for the IRS to take a chance of assessing a tax on someone not liable for one. That does not mean someone else at the IRS will not **assume** you are a taxpayer.

Section 6301. Collection authority

The Secretary shall collect the taxes imposed by the internal revenue laws.

It is time to let you know how the term "Secretary" is defined in the IRS Code. Notice that "Secretary" alone means either the 'secretary of the Treasury' <u>or</u>, his delegate.

Section 7701. Definitions
(11) Secretary of the Treasury and Secretary
(A) Secretary of the Treasury

The term "Secretary of the Treasury" means the Secretary of the Treasury, personally, and shall not include any delegate of his.

(B) Secretary

The term "Secretary" means the Secretary of the Treasury or his delegate.

If you read the other books that I have recommended, you will learn why you want to make sure that anyone who does anything against you at the IRS has the authority to act.

Please also note that, once again, this duty of the Secretary is in relation to taxes <u>imposed</u> by this title. Yes, I realize that I am belaboring the point regarding the fact that there <u>has</u> to be an imposition and duty imposed on you; I do it to stress how vital that point is. You must insist on knowing just where the liability begins. What statute imposed the duty on you? If there is no duty imposed, or tax imposed on you, then no one has the authority to collect your money under the guise of a tax. That is breaking the law.

If the Secretary had actually assessed you with a tax then he or she would have to do the following.

Section 6303. Notice and demand for tax
(a) General rule

Where it is not otherwise provided by this title, the Secretary shall, as soon as practicable, and within 60 days, after the making of an assessment of a tax pursuant to section 6203, give notice to each person liable for the unpaid tax, stating the amount and demanding payment thereof. Such notice shall be left at the dwelling or usual place of business of such person, or shall be sent by mail to such person's last known address.

I am including the next section to iterate that I personally, will never, ever, accept the appellation of "taxpayer" until the Government can show me just what section in the code (if there is any) which makes me liable for an Internal Revenue tax. When I read a code section like the one coming up and it says "taxpayer", I know that that section doesn't apply to me as I have not been made liable for a tax.

Section 6304. Fair tax collection practices
(a) Communication with the taxpayer

Without the prior consent of the taxpayer given directly to the Secretary or the express permission of a court of competent jurisdiction, the Secretary may not communicate with a taxpayer in connection with the collection of any unpaid tax—

Do you see that this section deals with and applies to taxpayers? It is time to look at liens and levies, which are of course, never fun. Even if you win you get beat up with the stress of it all! What does the government have to do to lien your property, or to "levy" it?

Section 6321. Lien for taxes

If any person liable to pay any tax neglects or refuses to pay the same after demand, the amount (including any interest, additional amount, addition to tax, or assessable penalty, together with any costs that may accrue in addition thereto) shall be a lien in favor of the United States upon all property and rights to property, whether real or personal, belonging to such person.

So what we see here is, again, the key phrase "liable to pay any tax" and then "refuses to pay." What if you insist you are not liable and that the government is in error as you are not **subject to** any Internal Revenue tax? Seems like you should have your day in court to dispute the liability, right?

Please look at section 6320 and see if this is the kind of hearing you want?

Section 6320. Notice and opportunity for hearing upon filing of notice of lien

(a) Requirement of notice

   (1) In general

   The Secretary shall notify in writing the person described in section 6321 of the filing of a notice of lien under section 6323.

   (2) Time and method for notice

   The notice required under paragraph (1) shall be—

(A) given in person;

(B) left at the dwelling or usual place of business of such person; or

(C) sent by certified or registered mail to such person's last known address, not more than 5 business days after the day of the filing of the notice of lien.

(3) **Information included with notice**

The notice required under paragraph (1) shall include in simple and nontechnical terms— ...

(b) **Right to fair hearing**

(1) **In general**

If the person requests a hearing under subsection (a)(3)(B), such hearing shall be held by the Internal Revenue Service Office of Appeals.

I don't know about you but this is not the hearing I want. First, it is a hearing for "taxpayers" run by the IRS and an 'impartial' agent who is impartial towards the IRS but <u>partial</u> against you. If things get this far, I am looking to find out how I can press my constitutional rights through the U. S. District Court which is not an '*executive*' branch court like the Tax Court. Would you ever go to a drug dealer hearing if you weren't a drug dealer? Then why would you go to a taxpayer hearing if you weren't one?

Remember, this book is not designed to go into depth on how to handle these sorts of things. Otto Skinner has accomplished this far better than I ever could. This book is designed to help get you out of the 'matrix' and to remove some tyranny from your mind.

The levy process is part and parcel to this lien process. Let's take a look at that now.

Section 6330. Notice and opportunity for hearing before levy
(a) Requirement of notice before levy
(1) In general

No levy may be made on any property or right to property of any person unless the Secretary has notified such person in writing of their right to a hearing under this section before such levy is made. Such notice shall be required only once for the taxable period to which the unpaid tax specified in paragraph (3)(A) relates.

Please take note that a levy is made in regards to unpaid taxes. This section presupposes that there is in fact a tax bill due and that the person is **subject to** and **liable fo**r an Internal Revenue tax. In other words a taxpayer.

(2) Time and method for notice

The notice required under paragraph (1) shall be—

(**A**) given in person;

(**B**) left at the dwelling or usual place of business of such person; or

(**C**) sent by certified or registered mail, return receipt requested, to such person's last known address; not less than 30 days before the day of the first levy with respect to the amount of the unpaid tax for the taxable period.

(3) Information included with notice

The notice required under paragraph (1) shall include in simple and nontechnical terms—

(b) Right to fair hearing
(1) In general

If the person requests a hearing under subsection (a)(3) (B), such hearing shall be held by the Internal Revenue Service Office of Appeals.

All of these statements of rules and regulations apply only to someone who is indeed subject to an internal revenue tax. <u>Not</u> to someone who is <u>not</u> **subject to** the IRS Code. Why would anyone who is <u>not</u> subject to the code accept any of these conditions?

> **Section 6331. Levy and distraint**
> **(a) Authority of Secretary**
> <u>If any person liable to pay any tax neglects or refuses</u> to pay the same within 10 days after notice and demand, it shall be lawful for the Secretary to collect such tax (and such further sum as shall be sufficient to cover the expenses of the levy) by levy upon all property and rights to property (except such property as is exempt under section 6334) belonging to such person or on which there is a lien provided in this chapter for the payment of such tax. Levy may be made upon the accrued salary or wages of any officer, employee, or elected official, of the United States, the District of Columbia, or any agency or instrumentality of the United States or the District of Columbia, by serving a   notice of levy on the employer (as defined in section 3401(d)) of such officer, employee, or elected official. If the Secretary makes a finding that the collection of such tax is in jeopardy, notice and demand for immediate payment of such tax may be made by the Secretary and, upon failure or refusal to pay such tax, collection thereof by levy shall be lawful without regard to the 10-day period provided in this section. [emphasis]

Notice the key words again "If any person **liable to pay** any tax neglects or refuses to pay" Although I am not from Missouri, I still want to be shown just where it is that I have been made liable for a tax.

Let's look at more in the same section. Here again the term "taxpayer" is key and since the whole code applies only to taxpayers and not to non taxpayers then all of this 'notice and appeals' information only applies to taxpayers and <u>not</u> to non taxpayers.

Now look at this great piece of work coming out of the IRC.

Section 6332. Surrender of property subject to levy

(a) Requirement

> Except as otherwise provided in this section, any person in possession of (or obligated with respect to) property or rights to property subject to levy upon which a levy has been made shall, upon demand of the Secretary, surrender such property or rights (or discharge such obligation) to the Secretary, except such part of the property or rights as is, at the time of such demand, subject to an attachment or execution under any judicial process.

Do you understand what they are saying here? I have never seen an IRS Levy, but I have seen IRS Notice of Levy many times. An IRS Notice of Levy is not a Levy but a notice only. From what I know a Levy is a judicial process. I conclude that all controversies are subject to judicial due process. This comes from our Constitution.

Amendment V

> No person shall be held to answer for a capital, or otherwise infamous crime, unless on a presentment or indictment of a Grand Jury, except in cases arising in the land or naval forces, or in the Militia, when in actual service in time of War or public danger; nor shall any person be subject for the same offence to be twice put in jeopardy of life or limb; nor shall be compelled in any criminal case to be a witness against himself, <u>nor be deprived of life, liberty, or property, without due process of law</u>; nor shall private property be taken for public use, without just compensation. [emphasis added]

What is "due process"? Well, I am sure it would have to start with there being an imposition of some sort of tax don't you agree? Then we would have to be made liable for that tax ("taxpayer"). Next someone with authority would have to assess that tax. So those are the three most important foundations before any collection activity could occur and that is just part of due process.

Section 6332. Surrender of property subject to levy
(c) Special rule for banks

Any bank (as defined in section 408 (n)) shall surrender (subject to an attachment or execution under judicial process) any deposits (including interest thereon) in such bank only after 21 days after service of levy

Seems like more of the same here. That is that government needs a judicial order to seize this property. But guess what, the banks usually turn the money over voluntarily. How nice for us.

Once again, this chapter was to inform not to solve the problem.

CHAPTER SEVEN

WHAT HAPPENS IF I AM INDICTED ON CRIMINAL CHARGES, &, HAS ANYONE WON AGAINST THE IRS ON INCOME TAX MATTERS?

If a criminal prosecution ever happens to you then I suggest, first and foremost, don't even consider getting into this position unless you either have to or are fully prepared to take the risk. And that means you better be well educated! If you get into this position for not paying an income tax, then, for heaven's sake, please don't be of the ilk that you think there is an income tax but you just don't want to pay. I am pretty sure that such a position will get you convicted.

It goes without saying that there are both civil and criminal prosecutions in regards to the Internal Revenue Code. None of which, I am afraid to tell you, in my opinion, are any fun. Of course, as for those of us who love to spit in 'tyranny's face', you may enjoy the process. I have yet to learn how to enjoy conflict.

I can't say this enough. Please read and re-read all three of Otto Skinner's books on this subject! "The Best Kept Secret," "The Biggest Tax Loophole of All,." and "If you are "The Defendant" It would also be an excellent idea to find and read the trial transcripts of Lloyd Long, Vernice Kuglin and Tommy Cryer. There are other transcripts worth reading in order to gain valuable information but with these cases you are going to learn how some winners did it.

Here are some of the things the government charges people with.

Section 7201. Attempt to evade or defeat tax

Any person who willfully attempts in any manner to evade or defeat any tax imposed by this title or the payment thereof shall, in addition to other penalties provided by law, be guilty of a felony and, upon conviction thereof, shall be fined not more than $100,000 ($500,000 in the case of a corporation), or imprisoned not more than 5 years, or both, together with the costs of prosecution.

I would hope that you would never attempt to willfully evade or defeat any tax imposed by the IRC. I hope that you always pay any and all taxes legally imposed on you. Having said that, I also hope that you will insist, before paying any tax, on finding out just where the tax is imposed, and how you became liable for it.

Now what does the IRS mean by "willfully" in the next statement? First, it means there must be a tax, and, that you are trying to defeat it or evade it with willfulness. Let's see what the Supreme Court has to say on this subject.

Cheek v. United States; Supreme Court of the United States, 1991 498 U.S. 192

"Willfulness, as construed by our prior decisions in criminal tax cases, requires   the <u>Government to prove that the law imposed a duty</u> on the defendant, that the <u>defendant knew of this duty</u>, and that <u>he voluntarily and intentionally violated that duty.</u> We deal first with the case where the issue is whether the defendant knew of the duty purportedly imposed by the provision of the statute or regulation he is accused of violating, a case in which there is no claim that the provision at issue is invalid. In such a case, if the Government proves actual knowledge of the pertinent legal duty, the prosecution, without more, has satisfied the knowledge component of the willfulness requirement. But carrying this burden requires negating a defendant's claim of ignorance of the law or a claim that, because of a misunderstanding of the law, he had a good-faith belief that he was not violating any of the provisions of the tax laws. This is so because one cannot be aware that the law imposes a duty upon him and yet be ignorant of it, misunderstand the law, or believe that the duty does not exist. In the end, the issue is whether, based on all the evidence, the Government has proved that the defendant was aware of the duty at issue, which cannot be true if the jury credits a good-faith misunderstanding and belief submission, whether or not the claimed belief or misunderstanding is objectively reasonable." [emphasis added]

So, I would think if you actually believe you have a duty to file and pay taxes, that you had better do it or you will likely lose in a criminal tax case. Please take note that willfulness is very important when it comes to tax crimes.

Section 7202. Willful failure to collect or pay over tax

Any person required under this title to collect, account for, and pay over any tax imposed by this title who willfully fails to collect or truthfully account for and pay over such tax shall, in addition to other penalties provided by law, be guilty of a felony and, upon conviction thereof, shall be fined not more than $10,000, or imprisoned not more than 5 years, or both, together with the costs of prosecution. [emphasis added]

Section 7203. Willful failure to file return, supply information, or pay tax

Any person required under this title to pay any estimated tax or tax, or required by this title or by regulations made under authority thereof to make a return, keep any records, or supply any information, who willfully fails to pay such estimated tax or tax, make such return, keep such records, or supply such information, at the time or times required by law or regulations, shall, in addition to other penalties provided by law, be guilty of a misdemeanor and, upon conviction thereof, shall be fined not more than $25,000 ($100,000 in the case of a corporation), or imprisoned not more than 1 year, or both, together with the costs of prosecution. In the case of any person with respect to whom there is a failure to pay any estimated tax; this section shall not apply to such person with respect to such failure if there is no addition to tax under section 6654 or 6655 with respect to such failure. In the case of a willful violation of any provision of section 6050I, the first sentence of this section shall be applied by substituting "felony" for "misdemeanor" and "5 years" for "1 year". [Emphasis added]

The next section is one I could be charged with if I ever made out an income tax return and signed it under the penalty of perjury. I am convinced that I am not liable or required to pay an income tax. Can you see how I could be charged with a crime if I signed a 1040 form and that I would be committing perjury?

Section 7206. Fraud and false statements
Any person who—

(1) Declaration under penalties of perjury
Willfully makes and subscribes any return, statement, or other document, which contains or is verified by a written declaration that it is made under the penalties of perjury, and which he does not believe to be true and correct as to every material matter; or

I think, without question, the following offenses are going on daily with tens of thousands of IRS agents across the country.

Section 7214. Offenses by officers and employees of the United States
(a) Unlawful acts of revenue officers or agents

Any officer or employee of the United States acting in connection with any revenue law of the United States—

(1) who is guilty of any extortion or willful oppression under color of law; or

(2) who knowingly demands other or greater sums than are authorized by law, or receives any fee, compensation, or reward, except as by law prescribed, for the performance of any duty; or ...

(3) who with intent to defeat the application of any provision of this title fails to perform any of the duties of his office or employment; or ...

(7) who makes or signs any fraudulent entry in any book, or makes or signs any fraudulent certificate, return, or statement; or

(8) who, having knowledge or information of the violation of any revenue law by any person, or of fraud committed by any person against the United States under any revenue law, fails to report, in writing, such knowledge or information to the Secretary; or

(9) who demands, or accepts, or attempts to collect, directly or indirectly as payment or gift, or otherwise, any sum of money or other thing of value for the compromise, adjustment, or settlement of any charge or complaint for any violation or alleged violation of law, except as expressly authorized by law so to do; ...

shall be dismissed from office or discharged from employment and, upon conviction thereof, shall be fined not more than $10,000, or imprisoned not more than 5 years, or both. The court may in its discretion award out of the fine so imposed an amount, not in excess of one-half thereof, for the use of the informer, if any, who shall be ascertained by the judgment of the court. The court also shall render judgment against the said officer or employee for the amount of damages sustained in favor of the party injured, to be collected by execution.

How many violations would an IRS agent be guilty of if they tried to get money out of you under the guise of a tax when in fact you are not liable? If this agent threatened you with jail or monetary penalties for something you did not owe would that not be extortion? If the agent failed to provide the section of the code that imposed a duty on you and then still insists that you hand over your money under the guise of a tax, would that be a chargeable offense?

If, from all of your studies, you were convinced that there was no imposition of any tax on you by Title 26 of the U.S. Codes (Internal Revenue Code), thus you decided not to falsely file tax forms, then you should certainly have a well documented history of your conclusions which would include all your correspondence with the IRS.

In this correspondence I would hope you will have years of documentation in regards to your Freedom of Information Act (F.O.I.A.) Requests and the resulting responses, or lack of responses, to your requests. Yes, I know you are dying to find out what such a paper trail should look like; that is why you need to buy Mr. Skinner's books. In one of those books "The Biggest Tax Loophole", he presents a fantastic example of a F.O.I.A. request.

Do you think it would serve your cause if you have years of documented requests to the IRS asking for the answer to a few simple questions such as 'Where, if at all, in the code have I been made **subject to** an 'Internal Revenue Code tax'? And, 'if I have a tax liability, please produce a copy of the "Record of Assessment" for me'.

It would not hurt anyone's cause to have expert opinions regarding the Internal Revenue Code, people who understand the fact that there is no place in the code that imposes a duty on you to pay an income tax regarding your labor and no obligation to keep books and records along with that. Expert opinions from lawyers and tax accountants are exceedingly valuable in a court of law.

Again, if you get to the point where you get indicted, the more knowledge you have the better. You also should make sure, if you do have lawyer, that he is trained in this area. If not, you might as well make a plea arrangement. There are only a few attorneys in the country who fully understand the true nature of the so-called "Income Tax"

You may even learn how to defend yourself, but you will have to work at learning this subject. Even lawyer Tommy Cryer, who won his case against the IRS, had another lawyer, Larry Becraft represent him. That may have something to do with the old saying that someone who represents himself has a fool for a client. But in tax matters, the client can also be a fool if he chooses an attorney who is ignorant of what you will have learned. (I think a lawyer who chooses to represent himself might not come across to the jury as being genuine or humble enough.)

Frankly, I don't believe that the government even has *'standing'* (jurisdiction) to bring you to court. ***Jurisdiction*** is not automatically granted to the U. S. District Court. Especially when there isn't a code section that makes you liable for a tax in the first place. Personal jurisdiction does not automatically convey to the U. S. District Court. There is plenty of information available on this subject and is, properly, the subject of another book. This is one of the reasons why I would never go to an IRS hearing or a Tax Court hearing as I don't ever want to do anything that would confer jurisdiction to the District Court. If the District Court, which is the same as the federal court, does not have jurisdiction, they can't try you.

If you sign any IRS document, volunteer any information, fail to refute false information or statements made by anyone, including IRS agents, or anyone from the public, it could harm you if you ever go to trial.

For me, one of the keys during this type of trial is to hold steadfast onto the idea that **the government has to prove that you are subject to a tax,** are liable for a tax, and, that you had income. If the defendant wants to try to prove why he or she does not owe or is not liable for a tax, and they present some theory to prove this, and their argument fails - then the jury may decide against them. Let the government try to 'prove the negative', don't take on that burden. Remember, if there is no section of the IR code that imposes a tax on you, then they can't produce one! I am not going to volunteer anything at any step of any proceeding. I am firmly convinced that I am not a taxpayer and that there is nothing in the code that imposes a duty on me, and that the IRS Code Title 26 does not apply to me any more than Title 25 (Indians) of the U. S. Code does. If the Executive branch of government, under Title 25, claimed I was subject to some obligation under that Title, not being an Indian (Native American), I would insist they show me how I became liable or subject to that Title. If they could not show me, I would not volunteer jurisdiction to them, or to the District Court, under that Title. I would move the court to dismiss the action due to the lack of 'personal' and 'subject matter' jurisdiction.

A motion to dismiss for lack of personal jurisdiction would go a long way to show a good faith belief that you were not subject to a tax and to negate the willfulness element needed to convict someone of a tax crime. If I believe that the code does not make me liable or subject to a tax, then why would I volunteer to have the court hear a criminal prosecution against me, when they can only get jurisdiction over me by an actual imposition of a tax on me?

Although there are many people who have won against the IRS, rest assured that neither the Media, nor the IRS, have any desire to let you know about those wins.

When you read Otto's books you will learn about Gail Sanocki, who wrote a brilliant motion that, not only stopped a sanity hearing that was scheduled by her court appointed attorney, an attorney who was supposed to assist her in her defense, but also got the whole indictment dismissed. Her motion covered areas of the law where she pressed her right to defend herself, along with her right to the assistance of counsel.

She demonstrated that her counsel was acting against her wishes and was indeed not any assistance at all.

The Trial of Lloyd Long was another victory for freedom, and a blow against tyranny. Lloyd Long was represented in his trial by Larry Becraft, a prolific attorney in the battle against IRS tyranny. It is my opinion that Lloyd Long won, mostly, because of his testimony and beliefs. A great deal of his testimony was devoted to the events he attended and the studying he completed in coming to his conclusions. He went into great detail as to what he had learned that led him to the conclusion that he was not required to pay an income tax and to file returns. He also presented, as evidence, a great many common sense questions that he had posed in writing to the IRS, and the utter nonsense, or non related answers, he got back. All of this went a long way, I have no doubt, in helping the jury to find Mr. Long not guilty.

Vernice Kuglin also bested the IRS in District Court. In her case, the jury instruction must have gone a long way in helping her win the case. 'Jury instructions', in my mind, are quite vital. *'The government must also prove beyond a reasonable doubt that the defendant acted willfully. A willful act is defined as a voluntary and intentional violation of a known legal duty. Thus, the government must prove beyond a reasonable doubt that the defendant possessed the specific intent to defeat or evade the payment of income tax the defendant knew it was her duty to pay.'*

Ms. Kuglin was a pilot with Federal Express. I tell you this to demonstrate that, because of her profession, she was most definitely a very capable and intelligent person. She was someone who understood her position regarding her non taxpayer status quite well. She, too, was represented by Larry Becraft.

Once again, it was shown in her trial that she did not come by her understanding lightly. She, like most of us in the country, **assumed** that we have to pay an income tax. Years of study and years of correspondence with the IRS, trying to get straight answers regarding income taxes, kept Ms. Kuglin free. Non-responsive answers are the norm with IRS agents. That does not help the IRS in court.

Joseph Bannister, a former IRS Agent, also bested the IRS in Court.

Mr. Bannister had researched the code and could not find the section that imposed an income tax on wages. He took this information to his superiors who only shunned him. When Agent Bannister got the cold shoulder from his superiors at the IRS, he did what any man of integrity would do, he quit.

Several years after his resignation, the IRS and the U.S. Department of Justice prosecuted Mr. Bannister. Mr. Bannister was acquitted; the main reason was that the jury did not find that Mr. Bannister possessed a willfulness to violate any IRC law/regulation.

Attorney Tommy Cryer, who was represented by Larry Becraft, submitted a motion for dismissal, which I found quite brilliant. His positions and points are about 90 % of what I would use. His emphasis was not on trying to prove why he was not subject to an income tax, but, instead, put the burden on government, to try and prove something they could not. Where is it, in the code, that he was made liable for an income tax?

Included in Mr. Cryer's proposed jury instructions was that a defendant can be found guilty of that offense only if all of the following facts are proved beyond a reasonable doubt:

> First: That the Defendant was required by law or regulation to make a return of his income for the taxable year charged;

> Second: That the Defendant failed to file a return at the time required by law; and;

> Third: That the Defendant's failure to file the return was willful.

If there is no law that imposes a duty on you, then it should be pretty hard for the government to get a conviction.

The following is a civil case win, regarding an IRS summons, by Bob Schulz. Quoting from the decision (***Schulz v. IRS*, Case No. 04-0196-cv),**

"...absent an effort to seek enforcement through a federal court, IRS summonses apply no force to taxpayers, and no consequence whatever can befall a taxpayer who refuses, ignores, or otherwise does not comply with an IRS summons until that summons is backed by a federal court order... [a taxpayer] cannot be held in contempt, arrested, detained, or otherwise punished for refusing to comply with the original IRS summons, no matter the taxpayer's reasons, or lack of reasons for so refusing."

Do you get that? If the IRS sends you a summons and you don't want to go, then you just politely refuse. They then will have to get the District Court to compel you to answer their summonses. And they can't punish you for not voluntarily complying with their so-called, "summons." Please notice again the word "taxpayer." Of course if a taxpayer has this protection, certainly a non taxpayer has more protections.

There are a lot more cases to study, both criminal and civil. However, this book is not intended to present an exhaustive list of cases, nor is it intended to make you think winning is easy. I believe there are reasons why some people win and some people lose. I think that the primary reason for winning is that you have been diligent by pressing the Government to provide answers to your questions and to keep putting the burden of proof on them. I think this is especially important for you to do during the years prior to any court action. This will leave you with a paper trail of all the non-responsive answers from the government and its agents.

Even though the government loves to publish all the times they crush the citizen in tax matters, I think it is important to find out why some lose, and some win. You should check out the loser section as well as the winner section, so you can be armed with what to do and what not to do. Please investigate these individuals as well.

Lynne Meredith
Art Farnsworth
Irwin Schiff
Richard Simkanin
Larkin Rose
Ed & Elaine Browne.

These are just a few names of people whose cases are worth studying. I personally know someone who was convicted of failure to file. He lost his case and did a one year prison term as he was totally ill prepared (or just plain overwhelmed). However, I believe even this was a small price to pay for liberty.

The whole point of this book is to lead you out of the matrix to some degree and to give you a little direction of where to go next.

Good luck and the best of freedom to you!

Mike Benoit

Epilogue

The Shame of this Tyranny

The worst part of all this tyranny upon the mind of man is the fact that most people in this country actually believe that this, so called, income tax is the price we pay for freedom. How in the world can slavery equal freedom? More importantly, how can anyone not call such a thing as an income tax, or any tax that claims a share of every hour of paid labor, enslavement?

This farce was foisted on us little by little. In the beginning only the super rich were sucked into this scheme. Each year a greater percentage of people were brought under this umbrella of tyranny. Since, in the beginning, only the very rich were nailed for this tax, the rest of us did not mind.

A little further down the track, the bracket for people who were sucked into this tyranny grew larger yet again. Then in a short while the government began to reach into the weekly paycheck of the working men and women of this country with social security deductions.

Then came WW II, and of course the assumption that the worker would owe income taxes at the end of the year was the order of the day, so the government had a good reason to withhold that tax just in case. They would return the tax if you did not owe at the end of the year. Many people thought of the tax refund as a boon to their pocket and even though it was their own money, they anticipated with great joy receiving their own money back.

The rich did not get particularly disturbed with the, so called, income tax because to a great degree they could pass the burden of the tax down the line to the people who ended up buying the products of the companies they owned, or, in the cost of the services they provided. The poor saw only the bounty of the redistribution presented by government who plundered on their behalf.

The vilest thing about such a system is that it creates a dependent on one end and a slave on the other. Mostly all of this is hidden from view. The average producer under this sort of system has no idea just how much of the tax burden falls on him.

INDEX